Revolt in the Congo
1960–64

An Interim History Book

Revolt In The Congo 1960–64

Edited by Howard M. Epstein

Facts on File, Inc.
119 West 57th Street, New York, N. Y.   10019

Revolt in the Congo

1960-64

TABLE OF CONTENTS

INTRODUCTION

The system of European colonial rule imposed on the African continent was shattered in 1960 by the mounting pressure of African nationalism. More than a dozen African nations were freed from British, French and Belgian tutelage during the year and formed their first independent governments. The transfer of power from the old colonial nations to the new African states was everywhere accompanied by some degree of social and political upheaval. In most of the new states, nationalist governments were able to contain post-independence tensions, but in a few cases the newly freed nations appeared to be heading toward a long period of unrest. In one of these, the former Belgian Congo, independence was the signal for mutiny in the armed forces and rebellion against the new central government.

The rebellion in the Congo threatened for a time to provoke massive foreign intervention and to make the new state another Cold War battleground. Belgium's troops remained in the country against the wishes of the Leopoldville government to protect Belgian nationals from Congolese rebels and mutinous troops. Belgian, British and French business interests openly supported the secessionist Katanga Province government led by Moise Tshombe. The USSR, Red China and East European Communist governments at first supported the militantly nationalist government of Congolese Premier Patrice Lumumba, and after his death backed the rebellion led from Stanleyville, a provincial capital, by Lumumba's followers.

The threat of full military intervention by East and West was diminished by the UN's decision to form an international force to restore order in the Congo and safeguard the new nation's independence. The UN military presence lasted for 4 years and was the most powerful single factor in the relative success of the Leopoldville government's efforts to stamp out the rebel and secessionist movements. When the last UN troops were withdrawn from the Congo, in June 1964, they left behind a Congo government that was weak but able increasingly to cope with the remaining armed opposition to its rule. The UN intervention was not, however, without cost; the UN's financial structure was seriously weakened by member states' refusals to pay their shares of the Congo peace-keeping costs; and Secy. Gen. Dag Hammarskjold met his death in an African plane crash in 1961 while flying to political talks with secessionist Katanga leaders.

This book is an unpolished, virtually day-to-day record of the Congolese rebellion and the events that flowed from it. It has been drawn from news reference materials provided by Facts on File and its associated publications, themselves compiled weekly from leading U.S. and foreign newspapers and press services. The editors have followed the pattern imposed by the original news dispatches, avoiding comment or bias, permitting the story to tell itself. As in all other volumes of the Interim History series, they have left the task of judgment to the reader.

1960

Belgium freed the Congo from colonial rule in 1960 under pressure of African nationalist agitation. An independent Congolese state was proclaimed and an elected government, headed by Premier Patrice Lumumba, took power. The new state was torn by army mutinies and political rebellion within days of its birth. The unrest brought a threat of Soviet intervention in the Congo against Belgium, which had refused to withdraw its troops, and implied counter-threats of action from the West. Foreign intervention was organized, but on an international scale, and a UN military force began arriving in the Congo within weeks. Even the UN military presence proved insufficient to cope with the rebellion, and the continued dissension led to Lumumba's forcible removal from power and his arrest by a government loyal to Congolese Pres. Joseph Kasavubu.

THE ROAD TO INDEPENDENCE

Belgium Signs Freedom Pacts

Belgian and African leaders reached agreement at a round-table conference in Brussels Jan. 20-Feb. 20, 1960 on terms for the establishment of an independent Congolese state. The Congo had been ruled by Belgium since 1885, when a Berlin Conference of European powers had recognized the existence of a "Congo Free State" as a personal fiefdom of the Belgian king, Leopold II. The king had relinquished responsibility for the Congo to the Belgian government in 1908, after an international scandal over abuses of the native populations, and since that date the country had been subject to governmental administration.

The Brussels conference was convened by Belgian Premier Gaston Eyskens for the announced purpose of discussing the Congo's future independence, not the form of the future Congolese government or its constitutional relationship to Belgium. But a formal pledge to hold Congolese elections, form a Congo government and end Belgian rule by June 30 was forced from Eyskens and Congo Minister Auguste de Schryver Jan. 27 after the African conferees refused to continue the talks on any other basis.

African leaders who successfully pressed the demands for swift formation of a Congolese government included Joseph Kasavubu and Daniel Kanza, president and vice president, respectively, of the Abako (Association of the Lower Congo), Moise Tshombe, president of the Katanga Province Conakat Party, Paul Bolya, head of the National Progress Party, and Patrice Lumumba, leader of the militant African nationalist faction of the Congolese National Movement. (Lumumba, who had been sentenced to 6 months in jail in Stanleyville Jan. 21 for inciting riots in Oct. 1959, was freed Jan. 25 to attend the Brussels talks.)

Dissension was evident among the African leaders attending the Brussels meeting: Lumumba urged a centralized Congolese state with a strong executive; Kasavubu favored a federal system under which the Abako could retain control of the lower Congo region; Tshombe and Bolya wanted the continuation of the Congo's close ties with Belgium through the establishment of strong political and economic links before independence.

A 16-point Congo independence program providing for the election of a bicameral Parliament and formation of a centralized Congo government before June 30 was completed at the conference Feb. 17. It was submitted to King Baudouin the next day and approved by the full conference Feb. 19. The Brussels talks ended Feb. 20.

Lumumba Party Wins First Election

The Congolese National Movement faction led by Patrice Lumumba emerged as the strongest Congolese political grouping in phased elections ending May 22 for the Congo's first Chamber of Representatives (later referred to as the National Assembly).

Final returns reported June 15 gave the militant Congolese National Movement (MNC) group 36 seats and the rival MNC faction led by Albert Kalonji 8 seats in the 137-member chamber.

The standings of other major parties: National Progress Party, 14 seats; African Solidarity Party, led by Antoine Gizenga, 13 seats; Kasavubu's Association of the Lower Congo (Abako), 12 seats; Cerea party, 10 seats; Tshombe's Conakat Party, 7 seats; Balubakat Party, 6 seats; African National Unity Party, 7 seats. Minor and regional parties divided the remaining 24 seats.

At least 25 deaths were reported in post-election violence in the Congo May 25-27. Kasavubu charged May 27 that Belgian officials had provoked Baluba-Lulua tribal unrest, in which 8 persons were killed in Kasai Province May 26, in order to prove the Congolese unprepared for self-government.

African Leaders Form Government

The country's first Congolese government came into existence June 24 with the confirmation of Patrice Lumumba as premier and the election of Joseph Kasavubu as president.

The government was formed as the result of a compromise under which Kasavubu, who had contested the premiership, accepted the presidency on condition the Abako party was given 3 cabinet posts. Major steps in formation of the government:

Resident Minister Walter Ganshof van der Meersch, named by Belgium May 16 to supervise the transfer of power in the Congo, called on Lumumba June 13 to explore the possibility of forming a cabinet. Lumumba announced June 14 that he had been pledged support of a majority in Parliament, but Congolese and Belgian opposition to him led van der Meersch to withdraw his mandate June 16.

Kasavubu was named premier-designate June 17, when the Congolese Parliament met for its inaugural session. He formed a provisional cabinet June 19 but was relieved of the post June 21 in the face of Lumumba's threats to form a separate government.

Lumumba was renamed premier June 21 after his faction of the Congolese National Movement had mustered a majority to elect Joseph Kasongo as president (speaker) of the lower house of Parliament. Lumumba formed a coalition cabinet and was confirmed in office June 23 by 74 of the 137 members of the Chamber of Representatives.

Kasavubu was elected Congolese president June 24 by a joint session of Parliament. He received 159 votes to 48 for Jean Bolikango, who had been the leader of efforts to form a majority opposed to Lumumba. Joseph Ileo, another leader of the anti-Lumumba group, was elected Senate president June 22. Kasavubu was sworn in as president June 27. (Kasavubu's Abako followers had proclaimed a general strike in Leopoldville June 23. They ended the walkout after his election.)

Congo Freed by Belgium

The Congo was proclaimed an independent republic June 30 in Leopoldville by King Baudouin.

In an address at the independence ceremonies, Baudouin expressed his "joy . . . that the Congo had acceded, . . . in full accord and friendship with Belgium, to independence and . . . sovereignty." Warning that the Congo's political and tribal divisions and its inexperience made it an "attraction" for "certain . . . foreign powers," Baudouin urged Congo leaders to seek Belgian aid in their work.

The ceremonies were marked by a speech in which Premier Lumumba lauded the "glorious history of our struggle for liberty" from the "humiliating slavery which had been imposed on us by force." Reminding Congolese of "the insults, the blows that we had to submit to . . . because we were Negroes," Lumumba called on them to make the Congo an effective democracy and the "rallying point of all Africa."

CIVIL STRIFE BEGINS

Tribesmen, Troops Mutiny

Severe civil strife broke out immediately following the Congo's release from Belgian rule.

Fighting began July 1 in Leopoldville and Luluabourg between rival Bakongo and Bakava tribesmen. At least 50 Africans were injured and 200 were arrested July 1-3 as troops fought disorders in both cities and imposed a nighttime curfew that ended independence celebrations.

Premier Lumumba warned July 3 that "the liberty we have just received does not mean license" and that order would be maintained. "We intend to safeguard the personal security and property of everyone—black or white—and . . . to be quite ruthless with lawbreakers," he declared.

A mutiny among Congolese troops demanding the removal of Belgian officers and immediate promotions began in Thysville July 5 and spread to Leopoldville the next day. Mutineers, who refused to accept Belgian orders and threatened to march against the government, surrendered their arms and released their officers in both cities July 7 in response to personal orders from Lumumba and Pres. Kasavubu. But Congolese troops seized control of Leopoldville and terrorized whites July 8 until Lumumba accepted demands for dismissal of all Belgians except advisers. The disorders spread July 9 to Katanga Province, where 2 Europeans were killed by mutinous African troops.

Maj. Gen. Emil Janssens, the Congolese Army's Belgian commander, resigned July 6 and was replaced July 9 by

Gen. Victor Lundula, a Congolese, who was promoted from sergeant-major to head the 25,000-man army.

A mass flight of Belgians and other Europeans began July 8 from the Congo to the neighboring (formerly French) Congo Republic, Northern Rhodesia, Uganda and Portuguese Angola. Thousands of whites crossed the Congo River on ferries from Leopoldville to neighboring Brazzaville; others boarded Belgian airliners which began refugee flights July 9 from Leopoldville to Brussels. Americans who had sought protection in the U.S. embassy in Leopoldville were removed by air beginning July 10. (U.S. Ambassador-to-Congo Clare H. Timberlake had turned back Congolese soldiers who sought to invade the embassy July 8 to seize an American photographer.) The white exodus was attributed to reports of rape and murder of Europeans by mutinous troops.

Belgian Forces Intervene in Strife

800 Belgian paratroops attacked rebellious Congolese soldiers in Elisabethville, Katanga Province July 10. Katanga Provincial Premier Moise Tshombe requested the Belgian intervention after the mutinous Congolese reportedly had killed 6 Europeans. 25 Congolese soldiers were reported to have been killed before the Belgians restored order in the city.

Other Belgian troops were parachuted into Luluabourg, Kasai Province to rescue besieged Europeans. Similar missions were carried out against mutinous Congo troops in Kitona, Matadi, Goma and Kabalo.

2,500 Belgian troops had remained in the Congo after the independence proclamation under Belgian-Congolese agreements. 240 more Belgian soldiers were airlifted to the Congo July 8, and orders for the dispatch of an additional 1,200 men were issued July 9 by Belgian Premier Eyskens.

Pres. Kasavubu welcomed the Belgian intervention July 10 and appealed to Belgian residents of the Congo to give the new state time "to restore the situation." Premier Lumumba, however, denounced the Belgian action the same day as based on "fallacious excuses" despite reports that the intervention had been requested formally by Congolese Foreign Min. Justin Bomboko.

Renewed fighting between Belgian and Congolese troops was reported in Leopoldville July 12 after 3 Congolese soldiers were killed by a rocket from a Belgian plane.

Katanga Province Secedes From Congo

The "total independence" of Katanga Province from the Congo was proclaimed July 11 by Katanga Premier Tshombe, who asked that Belgian troops remain in Elisabethville and that Belgian reinforcements be sent to other Katanga areas threatened by mutinying Congolese troops.

Premier Tshombe assailed the Lumumba government for alleged Communist tactics. He pledged strong ties between Belgium and "independent" Katanga, site of the Congo's huge copper and uranium mines. A request by Tshombe for troops and police from Northern Rhodesia was rejected by Britain July 11 on grounds that such a request was the responsibility of the central Congolese government. 50 Congolese mutineers were reported killed July 12 when Belgian troops attacked them in Jadotville, Katanga.

Lumumba and Kasavubu flew together to Elisabethville July 12 to persuade Tshombe to rescind the secession, but their plane was refused permission to land.

UN, U.S. Military Aid Sought

The central Congolese government, conceding its inability to suppress the spreading disorders, appealed to the United Nations July 10 and to the U.S. July 12 for assistance to reorganize its armed forces and repress the mutinies.

The appeal for UN military aid was made to UN Undersecy. Ralph Bunche in Leopoldville by Lumumba and Kasavubu. Bunche disclosed July 11 that he had assured the Congolese leaders of "as much assistance as possible" and had reported the request to UN Secy. Gen. Dag Hammarskjold, who flew from Geneva to UN headquarters in New York July 11 to discuss with UN delegates the possible dispatch of international aid to the Congo.

A Congolese cabinet request for U.S. troops to help

restore order in the Congo was disclosed July 12 in Leopoldville and at Pres. Dwight D. Eisenhower's Newport, R.I.
summer White House but was rejected by the U.S. on the
ground that the UN already was considering military assistance. A statement issued by White House Press Secy. James
C. Hagerty made it clear that no American troops would be
sent to the Congo either through "unilateral action" by the
U.S. or as part of a UN contingent. Pres. Eisenhower was
said to feel that military aid to the Congo should be extended only under UN auspices and should "not come from the
United States or any of the large Western nations."

(The request for U.S. troops reportedly was made by
Congolese cabinet members while Kasavubu and Lumumba
were away from Leopoldville on an unsuccessful mission to
restore order in the Luluabourg area.)

UN FORCE SENT TO CONGO

Security Council Acts On Appeal

A request by UN Secy. Gen. Hammarskjold for authority
to organize and send a UN Force to the Congo was approved
July 14 by the UN Security Council.

The Council was called into special session at UN headquarters in New York by Hammarskjold July 13 after he
had received urgent Congolese appeals for UN intervention
against the Belgian troops deployed in the Congo to protect
whites from Congolese attacks. The Congolese government
messages, circulated to the Council July 13, stressed "the
extremely urgent need" for the dispatch of a UN force to the
Congo. The Congolese government asked UN military aid
not to restore order in the Congo but rather "to protect the
national territory against . . . aggression . . . by Belgian
metropolitan troops."

Hammarskjold asked the Council to approve formation
of a UN Force for the Congo "with the utmost speed."
Although he refused to judge Belgium's purpose in maintaining its forces in the Congo, he expressed the view that the
Belgian units were a source of "internal and . . . international tension" and would best be replaced by UN-commanded
troops. Hammarskjold made clear that the UN Force (1)

would include African troops but not those of the great powers, (2) "would not be authorized to action beyond self-defense" and (3) would not be a "party to internal conflicts in the country."

A resolution embodying Hammarskjold's request was introduced July 13 by Tunisian Amb.-to-UN Mongi Slim and was approved by the Council July 14 by an 8-0 vote (Britain, France and Nationalist China abstaining). The resolution called on the Belgian government "to withdraw their troops from the territory of the Republic of the Congo." It specifically authorized Hammarskjold to give the Congo "military assistance . . . until, through the efforts of the United Nations," Congolese forces were "able . . . to meet fully their tasks."

Belgian delegate Walter Loridan told the Council July 14 that Belgian troops would be withdrawn from the Congo when the UN Force provided "effective" restoration of order.

The Council session was marked July 13 by accusations exchanged between Soviet delegate Arkady A. Sobolev and U.S. Amb.-to-UN Henry Cabot Lodge. Sobolev charged that the U.S. and other Western states, acting in accord with Belgium, had tried to undermine the sovereignty of "the fledgling Congolese state." He asserted that Congolese army mutinies had been provoked by Belgian officers and a "panic" organized by "large industrial monopolies" in order to justify armed intervention in the Congo by Belgium with the aid of the U.S. and Britain. Lodge replied that Sobolev's "outrageous and untrue statements" were part of the usual Soviet effort to advance its cause by "making every bad situation worse."

International Force Established

An appeal by Hammarskjold for troop contributions for a UN Force in the Congo brought pledges of men July 14 from Ghana, Guinea, Ethiopia, Morocco, Tunisia and the Mali Federation. The U.S., Britain and other Western nations offered assistance with transportation, communications and supplies.

The plan to form and send a UN Force to the Congo

had been worked out by Hammarskjold at a meeting with Security Council representatives July 13.

Sweden's Maj. Gen. Carl Carlsson von Horn, chief of staff of the UN Truce Supervision Organization in Israel and the Arab states, was appointed by Hammarskjold July 14 to command the UN Force. Von Horn, accompanied by a small staff drawn from the UNTSO, arrived in Leopoldville to assume his post July 18. Hammarskjold July 15 named UN administrator Virgil DeAngelis to head a UN Force staging area in Kano, Nigeria, and Henry R. Labouisse, former director of the UN Relief & Works Agency for Palestine refugees, as his (Hammarskjold's) special assistant for the UN Force.

UN Undersecy. Bunche was named July 15 to serve as interim commander of the UN Force until von Horn's arrival. He was assisted by Maj. Gen. Henry Templar Alexander, a British officer serving as chief of Ghana's Defense Staff. Sture Linner, a Swedish businessman, was named by Hammarskjold July 15 as his personal representative in charge of UN technical assistance to the Congo.

UN Troops Arrive in Congo

Troop contingents for the UN Force began arriving in the Congo July 15 from Ghana and Tunisia aboard U.S. and British transport planes. Units from Morocco and Ethiopia landed July 16.

In the first action undertaken by the UN military staff, Gen. Alexander July 15 negotiated an agreement with Congolese soldiers in Leopoldville to remain in their camp near the city on condition Belgian forces did not move out of their positions dominating the city's main highways and airport. The accord was broken the same day when Alexander called on Congolese troops to restore order after a mob had formed in Leopoldville.

The UN Force began patrols in and around Leopoldville July 16. It supervised joint units of Belgian soldiers and Congolese police detailed by Alexander to disperse Congolese civilians protesting the Belgian refusal to leave the Congo. (It was reported July 16 that Belgian troop reinforcements were continuing to arrive in Leopoldville from Europe. 2 Belgian planes were reported to have been shot down outside Leopoldville by Congolese soldiers July 17.)

In his first report on the UN operation to the Security Council, Hammarskjold disclosed July 18 that Belgian officials in the Congo had agreed to accept UN Force orders and to limit their troops' actions to "the security . . . of Belgian nationals." Hammarskjold said that 3,500 African troops and 625 Swedish troops from the UN Emergency Force in the Gaza Strip had joined the UN command in the Congo. The Africans consisted of 460 Ethiopians, 770 Ghanaians, 1,250 troops from Morocco and 1,020 from Tunisia.

Belgians Continue Attacks

Belgian troops in the Congo seized control of key areas of Leopoldville, killing 6 Congolese soldiers in a fight for the city's airport, and continued their deployment throughout the country July 13 in an effort to protect whites against marauding Congolese. The Belgians took the Leopoldville airport after Congolese had fired on convoys of white refugees on their way to evacuation by plane. Congolese officials charged July 14 that 10 Congolese soldiers had been killed in Leopoldville when Belgian troops tricked them into joint security patrols, then tried to disarm them.

The military moves were carried out despite demands July 12 by Pres. Kasavubu and Premier Lumumba that Belgian forces halt their attacks and return to the bases provided them under Belgian-Congolese military agreements. Belgian Defense Min. Arthur Gilson said July 13 that the Belgian forces would continue their mission of "assuring protection everywhere" in the Congo.

In a 2-hour address to the Congolese Parliament July 15, Premier Lumumba renewed his demands for the "immediate withdrawal" of Belgian troops and demanded the recall of Belgian diplomatic representatives from the Congo. Lumumba told Parliament that Belgian forces were carrying out a plan to overthrow the Congolese government. He charged that Belgian officials had tried to sabotage his

mission to restore order in other parts of the Congo and
that he and Pres. Kasavubu had been jeered, jostled and
spat upon by Belgians at Leopoldville airport July 14.
He warned that "to save the nation, we are ready to
make a pact with the devil himself."

(The State Department confirmed July 14 that American missionaries had been ordered to leave Congo danger
areas. The department broadened the evacuation order
July 15 to include all 1,700 U.S. missionaries in the
country.)

USSR THREATENS INTERVENTION

Khrushchev Warns Belgians

In the first major Soviet statement to be issued on the
Congo, Premier Nikita S. Khrushchev said at a Moscow
news conference July 12 that Belgium, with the connivance
of NATO, was "sending troops to suppress the people of
the Congo by force of arms" on the "pretext of alleged
disorder there while in fact real order is being introduced."
"The people of the Congo," he said, "want to establish
genuine order, to expel colonialists." "The colonial peo-
ples fighting for their freedom and independence have our
sympathies and our assistance," he declared.

Soviet notes delivered July 13 to the U.S., Britain,
France, Belgium and West Germany reiterated the Khrushchev charges and demanded that the UN "put an end to
the aggression" committed by Belgium in the Congo. The
USSR asserted that Congolese disorders had been caused
by "Belgian officers" who "provoked armed incidents in
a number of camps for African soldiers" to justify the
Belgian troops' intervention.

A Belgian note to the USSR rejected with "contempt"
July 15 the Soviet demand for a Belgian troop withdrawal.
It said that "horrible disorders" had been provoked in
the Congo by the new state's army and that the Congolese
government had been "unable to stop them or control
them." Belgium asserted that "no country could have
abstained from its sacred duties . . . to protect its com-
patriots in extreme danger."

Congo Appeals For Red Support

A Congolese government appeal July 14 for Soviet aid against Belgium was accepted the next day by the USSR with a warning to the West to keep "hands off" the Congo.

The Congolese appeal, signed by Pres. Kasavubu and Premier Lumumba, asked the USSR to "watch hourly" over the Congo in view of the threat "from Belgium and certain Western countries supporting Belgium's conspiracy against our independence." "It is possible," the Congolese declared, "that we may have to ask for the Soviet Union's intervention should the Western camp not stop its aggression."

A reply cabled by Khrushchev and made public with the Congolese appeal July 15 warned that if the Western powers continued their "criminal actions, the USSR will not shrink from resolute measures to curb the aggression." It said that the Congo could be assured that the USSR would give "the necessary help which may be required for the victory of your just cause." The State Department denounced the Khrushchev message July 15 as "misleading" and "another example of the current Soviet attempt to inflame the international atmosphere."

A warning that the Congolese government would appeal for assistance from "Soviet Russian troops" unless Belgian troops withdrew from the Congo within 72 hours was transmitted by Premier Lumumba July 17 to Maj. Gen. Alexander, acting UN Force commander. Lumumba's ultimatum contained the draft of a formal Congolese request for Soviet military aid against Belgium. It was repudiated by the Congolese Senate, however, with the unanimous adoption July 18 of a resolution forbidding Soviet military intervention in the Congo.

A communique issued by Lumumba July 20 said the Congo cabinet had decided "to appeal immediately to the Soviet Union or any other country of the Asian-African bloc to send troops to the Congo" unless the UN Force began determined action to force a Belgian withdrawal from the Congo. Lumumba said the troops would be used to "peacefully bring about the evacuation of Belgian forces," restore internal order and "prevent all aggression from outside" the country.

UN Bars Foreign Involvement

The threat of intervention in the Congo by troops of Soviet-bloc or other foreign countries brought a UN Security Council appeal July 22 against any action that might aggravate the strife.

The Security Council appeal was contained in a resolution adopted unanimously after a 2d round of debate July 20-22 on the Congolese situation. The resolution, introduced July 21 by Tunisia and Ceylon, (1) called on Belgium to implement the withdrawal of its troops and authorized Secy. Gen. Hammarskjold "to take all necessary action to this effect"; (2) requested "all states to refrain from any action which might tend to impede the restoration of law and order" or "undermine the territorial integrity and the political independence of the Republic of the Congo."

The Council had been convened July 20 to discuss the Congo situation and hear Hammarskjold report on formation of the UN Force. He reported that the force comprised 12 battalions of African troops and 2 battalions of European troops and had attained a "satisfactory basis" in all areas of the Congo except Katanga.

Thomas Kanza, 27, Congolese envoy, charged July 20 that Belgium had broken its treaty of friendship with the Congo by ordering its soldiers into action against Congolese troops and civilians without consulting the Congolese government. He accused Belgium of provoking the attempted secession of Katanga Province.

Belgian Foreign Min. Pierre Wigny replied July 20 that Belgian troops in the Congo had intervened "because of a sacred duty of protecting the life and honor of our fellow citizens" after Congolese officials had shown themselves "incapable of restoring order" and after "appeals of violence and . . . massacre" had spread through the Congo. Wigny said: "As soon as the United Nations troops arrive in sufficient number, . . . then and to the same extent, we are prepared to withdraw."

Soviet First Deputy Foreign Min. Vasily Kuznetsov denounced Belgium July 20-21 for its armed interference in the Congo and for attempting to reimpose the "colonialist yoke" on the new state.

U.S. Amb.-to-UN Lodge, referring to Soviet threats of intervention in the Congo, warned July 21 that, with other UN members, "we will do whatever may be necessary to prevent the intrusion of any military forces not requested" by the UN.

Belgium Ends Buildup of Forces

The Belgian government admitted July 20 that it had continued sending military forces to the Congo despite its announced agreement to UN requests for the withdrawal of its troops as soon as possible. Belgium said that it had ended the movement of troops to the Congo.

The Belgian admission was made after a C-119 transport had crashed near Goma, in the eastern Congo, earlier July 20 while en route from Brussels with reinforcements. 34 soldiers were killed in the crash.

The complete withdrawal of Belgian troops from Leopoldville and most other major Congo cities outside Katanga Province was announced by Belgium July 23. The troops were withdrawn to the Kitona base area to await transportation home, although some soldiers were to remain at Kitona pending a final disposition of the base.

LUMUMBA VISITS UN TO PLEAD CASE

Mission Wins Pledges of Aid

Congolese Premier Lumumba left Leopoldville July 22 and flew to the U.S. via Accra and London to seek economic and political support for his dissension-torn country from the UN, U.S. and Canada.

Meeting with newsmen before his departure from Leopoldville, Lumumba retracted his threat to call for armed Soviet intervention in the Congo. He said that if Belgium withdrew its troops from the Congo—including its treaty bases at Kamina and Kitona—and recalled its ambassador, there would be no need for any but Congolese and UN forces in the country. Lumumba said, however, that Belgians had built the Congo, were "our friends" and would participate in future development of the Congo.

During a brief London stopover July 23 for talks with British officials, Lumumba had told newsmen that he was "not a Communist" and could be described best as a nationalist.

Lumumba arrived in New York July 24, and began immediate talks with Secy. Gen. Hammarskjold on possible expansion of UN efforts to quell Congo disorders. Lumumba said at a UN news conference July 25 that (1) Belgian troops must leave the Congo entirely; (2) Hammarskjold would negotiate a withdrawal deadline during a visit to Brussels; (3) his government's foreign policy was based on "positive neutralism"; it sought "contacts with all nations," including the Soviet Union, and (4) UN troops would be asked to remain in the Congo after the Belgians' departure to complete the restoration of order and to reorganize the Congolese armed forces.

A joint communique issed by Hammarskjold and Lumumba July 26 at the end of their talks pledged the UN's "immediate dispatch to the . . . Congo of technical assistance personnel" in "fields of administration and security." The communique reported Lumumba's "insistence that the reestablishment of peace in the Congo was conditioned on the immediate departure of Belgian troops."

Lumumba flew to Washington July 27 for talks with State Secy. Christian A. Herter. In statements made after the talks, Herter pledged an unspecified amount of U.S. technical and economic aid for the Congo through the UN, and Lumumba declared his satisfaction with the promise. He told newsmen the Congo would accept aid from the U.S. and "any other countries which are ready to help" with no "ulterior motives."

Lumumba, addressing a Negro audience at Howard University, urged July 27 that "students of this university send to Africa, to help their ancestors, dentists and doctors and engineers with all possible skills." During a press conference held July 28 in Washington, after he had met with Pres. Eugene R. Black of the International (World) Bank, Lumumba said that he would welcome "American or other" forces in the Congo. He left Washington for Canada July 29 after charging, in an airport statement, that "the whole of Africa" was "threatened by Belgium."

Arriving in Montreal July 29, Lumumba denied charges made July 28 by a Belgian royal commission that 291 white women had been raped by marauding Congolese troops. He claimed that an inquiry conducted by Belgian jurists for the Congo government had failed to substantiate a single rape charge. Lumumba conferred July 30 with Canadian Prime Min. Diefenbaker, but he failed to obtain more than a promise that Canada would provide some aid for the Congo through the UN. He returned to New York July 30.

In a letter transmitted to Security Council Pres. Armand Berard of France Aug. 1, Lumumba charged that Belgium had refused to comply with UN demands for the withdrawal of its troops. Lumumba said: the Belgian "intention is to disorganize the country" and cause "economic and financial difficulties"; "there is now no justification whatever for the presence of Belgian military forces in the Congo"; UN troops and "our national army are fully adequate to insure the maintenance of order."

Lumumba left New York Aug. 2 en route to a series of meetings with African leaders. He conferred with Tunisian Pres. Habib Bourguiba in Tunis Aug. 3, with King Mohammed V of Morocco in Rabat Aug. 4-5, Guinean Pres. Sekou Toure in Conakry Aug. 6, Liberian Pres. Willaim V.S. Tubman in Monrovia Aug. 7, and Ghanaian Pres. Kwame Nkrumah in Accra Aug. 8. He returned to Leopoldville Aug. 8.

KATANGA PROVINCE BARS UN FORCE

Hammarskjold Flies to Congo

UN Secy. Gen. Hammarskjold left New York July 27 on a personal mission to Belgium and the Congo for talks on the delayed deployment of UN troops in Katanga Province. Katanga, the site of most of the Congo's huge copper mines and other mineral wealth, had refused to permit UN forces to replace the Belgian troops supporting its secessionist government.

Meeting with Belgian Premier Gaston Eyskens' cabinet in Brussels July 27, Hammarskjold read to it the Security Council resolution demanding a speedy withdrawal of Belgian troops from all parts of the Congo. But he failed to win a

Belgian pledge of compliance with the UN demands. At a press conference held after their talks with Hammarskjold, Eyskens, Foreign Min. Pierre Wigny and Defense Min. Arthur Gilson declared that Belgian troops would remain in Katanga and any other areas where the UN failed to give sufficient protection to threatened Europeans. They made clear that Belgian troops would withdraw only to their treaty bases of Kamina and Kitona and would not leave the Congo until the bases' future had been decided by negotiation.

Hammarskjold flew July 28 to Brazzaville, capital of the (former French) Congo Republic, and entered neighboring Leopoldville later that day. He met with the Congolese cabinet July 30. In an address at a reception for Hammarskjold July 31, Deputy Premier Antoine Gizenga charged that the UN had helped Belgium in "a war of colonial reconquest."

Negotiated UN Entry Fails

Premier Tshombe's separatist Katanga government rejected Hammarskjold's attempt to negotiate the entry of UN troops into the province and forced him Aug. 5 to cancel orders for the deployment to begin.

In a statement issued Aug. 2 in Leopoldville, Hammarskjold said that UN Undersecy. Bunche would begin talks in Katanga on the withdrawal of Belgian troops from the province and that UN Force contingents would enter Katanga Aug. 6 to assume control of positions evacuated by the Belgians. He said Belgium had given assurances that its troops would cooperate with the entering UN Force.

Tshombe, who had warned that UN troops would be resisted by force, ordered the mobilization of all able-bodied Katanga men Aug. 3 to oppose the threatened UN troop move. In a statement issued after a Katanga cabinet meeting, Tshombe warned that "the Katanga government is unanimous in its will to resist by all means the Lumumba government . . . and the UN troops. Their arrival will be the signal for a general uprising." Katangans began reporting to military camps Aug. 4 for training.

Hammarskjold, in a clarifying statement made in Leopoldville Aug. 3, asserted that "the entry of United Nations troops into Katanga . . . in no way constitutes interference . . . in the internal affairs of the . . . province." Hammarskjold stressed that UN troops were under his personal control and could not be used to carry out orders of any government, including that of the Congo.

Bunche arrived in Elisabethville, the capital of Katanga, Aug. 4 and was rebuffed by Tshombe in efforts to win agreement for a peaceful entry of UN forces into the province. Tshombe told reporters after their meeting that he had warned Bunche that if UN troops tried to force their way into Katanga, they would be resisted. A test landing of 21 UN civilian technicians at Elisabethville airport was frustrated Aug. 5 when Katanga Interior Min. Godefroid Munongo forced their plane to return to Leopoldville without unloading. Bunche, who was at the airport when the plane landed, returned with it.

The cancellation of the UN move into Katanga was issued by Hammarskjold Aug. 5 after Bunche arrived in Leopoldville and told him that UN troops could not enter the province without causing bloodshed. Hammarskjold left Leopoldville for New York Aug. 5 after announcing that he had called a Security Council meeting to review the Katanga situation. In a report transmitted to the Council Aug. 6, Hammarskjold outlined the situation in the Congo and Katanga and said that the Council had 2 possible choices of action: (1) to alter the mandate of the UN Force to permit it to fight its way into Katanga, an action that Hammarskjold termed "impossible," or (2) to give Katanga authorities strong assurances that the presence of the UN force would not undermine their campaign against rule by the central Congo government.

(Tshombe's position as leader of the secessionist Katanga regime was confirmed Aug. 8 when the Katanga Provincial Assembly unanimously elected him "chief of state." The session, attended principally by members of Tshombe's Conakat Party, was boycotted by the opposition Katanga Cartel, known also as the Balubakat Party. A new Katanga Constitution, providing for an independent government based on an elected Chamber of Representatives and an advisory High Council of Chiefs had been approved by the Assembly Aug. 5.)

Leopoldville Threatens Invasion

The delay in the entry of UN troops into Katanga brought threats of an invasion of the province by troops of the central Congolese government.

Premier Lumumba had warned Hammarskjold in a cable from Rabat Aug. 5 that his government would take action if the UN Force did not immediately replace Belgian troops in Katanga. Lumumba recalled all Congolese troops to active service Aug. 9 and said at a news conference that he would lead the army into Katanga "ready to fight or die." The Congo cabinet decreed a state of emergency throughout the country Aug. 9, and Lumumba warned that Gen. Victor Lundula, army commander-in-chief, had been given "full powers" to suppress threats to the Congolese state. In a strong attack on the activities of Catholic priests and missionaries, Lumumba warned he would strike against the "secessionist movements" and the "Catholic imperialists" backing them.

Council Orders UN Troops to Move

The Security Council Aug. 9 ordered UN troops sent into secessionist Katanga Province to replace the Belgian troops maintained there in defiance of UN resolutions.

The Council acted after Secy. Gen. Hammarskjold had requested assurances for Katanga that the presence of UN forces would not prejudice the province's campaign for independence. Meeting in New York, the Council voted Aug. 9 by 9-0 (Italy and France abstaining) to adopt a Tunisian-Ceylonese resolution containing these major provisions: (1) A renewed demand for "speedy modalities" for the withdrawal of Belgian armed forces from all parts of the Congo, including Katanga, and their replacement by UN forces. (2) A declaration that "the entry of the United Nations Force into the Province of Katanga is necessary for the full implementation of this resolution." (3) A reaffirmation that "the United Nations Force in the Congo will not be a party to or in any way intervene or be used to influence the outcome of any internal conflict. . . . "

Hammarskjold, convening the Council session Aug. 8, warned that rapid "solution of the Congo problem is a question of peace or war"—a war not limited to the Congo. Hammarskjold appealed for Council action to clarify his mandate in the Congo and to make clear to the contending groups in the Congo and Katanga that the UN did not seek to impose a settlement of their differences. He told the Council that Tshombe's Katanga government had "organized military opposition . . . against the entry of the United Nations Force" and that "such opposition would require military initiative" for which he would need Council authorization. Hammarskjold asserted that compliance with UN resolutions by all parties to the Congo crisis would obviate the need for force.

Hammarskjold rejected a Soviet draft resolution that would have ordered the UN Force to use "any means" to "remove" Belgian troops from Katanga and the Congo. He said that the UN would not "help the Congolese people by actions in which Africans kill Africans or Congolese kill Congolese." Hammarskjold denied charges by Soviet First Deputy Foreign Min. Vasily V. Kuznetsov that the UN Force had disarmed Congolese troops but had failed to carry out its mandate to replace Belgian forces and calm public unrest. The Soviet resolution was withdrawn by Kuznetsov Aug. 9 before the vote on the Tunisian-Ceylonese resolution embodying the requests made by Hammarskjold.

Other statements before the Council Aug. 8: Congolese Foreign Min. Justin Bomboko charged that the Katanga government's refusal to admit UN Forces was the result of "an opposition created and maintained by the Belgian government"; Belgian Foreign Min. Wigny asserted that (a) Katanga authorities would admit UN troops as soon as they had received assurances of the UN's intent, and (b) Belgian forces would be withdrawn as soon as the safety of Belgian nationals was assured; U.S. Amb.-to-UN Lodge said that the UN must not become involved in the conflict between Congolese and Katanga authorities but that the UN Force should enter Katanga to permit a "speedy withdrawal" of Belgian troops.

UN TROOPS ENTER KATANGA

Hammarskjold Leads Contingent

Secy. Gen. Hammarskjold led an advance guard of 240 Swedish troops of the UN Force into Katanga Province Aug. 12. The UN move was carried out under an agreement reached in an exchange of cabled messages Aug. 10 between Hammarskjold and Katanga Pres. Tshombe. Hammarskjold's cable informed Tshombe that he would arrive in Elisabethville with Gen. Ben Hammou Kattani of Morocco, UN Force deputy commander, Brig. I. J. Rikhye of India, Hammarskjold's military adviser in the Congo, and "2 companies of the Swedish battalion" of the UN Force. Hammarskjold, who told Tshombe that he could not, under the Security Council's Aug. 9 resolution, negotiate conditions for the UN's entry into Katanga, said that the troops would be "under my exclusive personal authority and will have only the right of legitimate self-defense in the event—which I rule out as inconceivable—that they are attacked."

Tshombe's message expressed hope that their meeting would "insure respect for the territorial sovereignty of my government and the free exercise of its rights." Tshombe, however, warned Aug. 11 that the UN would be violating its pledges of nonintervention in Katanga if its presence "led to the arrival here of emissaries" of the central Congolese government.

Hammarskjold flew from New York to Leopoldville Aug. 11 and left for Elisabethville the next day, accompanied by the Swedish troops in 8 UN-marked transport planes. Their arrival was delayed briefly when Hammarskjold was informed that only his plane would be permitted to land, but all 8 craft were given personal clearance by Tshombe after Hammarskjold had threatened to order all of the planes to return to Leopoldville.

The UN contingent began assuming guard duties from Belgian soldiers Aug. 13 under a series of agreements negotiated and made public that day by Hammarskjold and Tshombe. 3 communiques issued by them: (1) reaffirmed the "principle of non-interference in internal affairs which applies to the activities of such a force"; (2) announced Belgian-UN agreement on the withdrawal of Belgian troops to their Kamina treaty base, the assumption of Belgians' duties by UN troops to arrive Aug. 15-16, and plans for talks on Belgian withdrawal from the Kamina base; (3) announced that the Swedish troops would assume control of the Elisabethville airport immediately.

The Swedish UN troops brought to Katanga by Hammarskjold were reinforced by more than 1,000 men Aug. 15; Moroccan and Swedish contingents were flown to Elisabethville and Mali Federation units were sent to Albertville, eastern Katanga, by train. 700 more troops were added to the Katanga force Aug. 16; the principal element was an Ethiopian battalion flown to Kamina.

A declaration issued Aug. 13 by the Katanga government said that the agreements had left it "complete freedom" of "all the political and administrative prerogatives for the maintenance of the present structures" of the Katanga regime, including "rights of internal police in the entire territory."

(In a report Aug. 12 to the Security Council, Hammarskjold outlined the UN's policy of non-intervention in the Congo and Katanga and made it clear that UN troops could not be used "to subdue or force the provincial government to a specific line of action" desired by the central government. Citing the example of the UN's neutral intervention in Lebanon in 1958, Hammarskjold said the UN Force would not transport or protect central government personnel attempting to enter Katanga, beyond "its . . . duty to maintain law and order," but neither would it halt the central government from taking "any action which by their own means . . . they can carry through in relation to Katanga." Hammarskjold's report also detailed a program of UN aid for the Congo that would go far beyond ordinary technical assistance programs or the Operational & Executive Personnel (OPEX) program created by the UN to aid inexperienced governments. Under the Congo aid plan, a Consultative Group of "senior experts," headed by Sture C. Linner of Sweden, was formed to give guidance to the Leopoldville regime.

Belgian Troops Leave Katanga

The Belgian military presence in Katanga was ended formally Aug. 14 by Gen. Roger A. Gheysen, commander of Belgian forces in the Congo, at Elisabethville ceremonies attended by Tshombe, Maj. Gen. von Horn, Swedish commander of the UN Force, Count Harold d'Aspremont Lynden, personal representative of Belgian Premier Eyskens, and an emotional crowd of Belgians and Congolese.

Control of Elisabethville was turned over to von Horn later that day, and Belgium's 1,600 troops in Katanga withdrew to the Kamina base area Aug. 15-16. Swedish UN troops were sent to Jadotville, 65 miles northwest of Elisabethville, Aug. 14 after 3 Congolese had been killed and several had been wounded there Aug. 13 in clashes between police and Lumumba supporters.

Hammarskjold flew to the Kamina base Aug. 14 en route to Leopoldville and discussed with Belgian officials the withdrawal of troops assembled at the base from other Congo areas. A Belgian statement issued later in the day said that only the withdrawal of troops normally based elsewhere in the Congo had been discussed and that garrison troops would remain at the base until its future had been decided by negotiations. Hammarskjold left Leopoldville for New York Aug. 15.

Lumumba Demands Katanga Control

A new Security Council meeting was called by Hammarskjold Aug. 15 as a result of threats by Lumumba to launch an invasion of Katanga and to expel white UN troops from the Congo unless the UN made Katanga accept the authority of the central government.

Lumumba, who had denounced Hammarskjold Aug. 13 for picking white troops to spearhead the UN's entry into Katanga, declared in a note to Hammarskjold Aug. 14 that his "neutral" use of UN troops in Katanga and his "connivance" with Katanga authorities were violations of his Security Council orders to "place all its resources at my command." Lumumba's message, delivered to Hammarskjold Aug. 15, said that "contrary to your personal interpretation, the United Nations Force may be used to subdue the rebel government of Katanga," and "has the duty" to transport Congolese government representatives to Katanga and protect them in their work.

Lumumba charged that Hammarskjold's negotiations with Tshombe had made the UN "a party to the conflict" between the 2 governments. He demanded that the UN: (1) turn over control of all airfields to Congolese troops; (2) send to Katanga a mixed force of Congolese and African UN contingents; (3) transport Congolese government representatives to Katanga; (4) disarm troops of the secessionist Katanga government and turn their arms over to troops of the central Congolese government; (5) withdraw all "non-African" troops from Katanga.

Hammarskjold Aug. 15 denounced Lumumba's "unfounded and unjustified allegations" concerning his interpretation of the UN Force mandate and said that he would seek further Security Council clarification of the UN's role in the Congo. Lumumba replied later in the day that the Congo had "lost confidence" in Hammarskjold. He demanded that the UN send to the Congo observers drawn from Asian and African states to insure implementation of its decisions.

UN Reaffirms Force's Neutrality

The Security Council indorsed Secy. Gen. Hammarskjold's neutral use of the UN Force by refusing, in an emergency session in New York Aug. 21-22, to alter or restrict the mandate it had given Hammarskjold to deal with the Congo situation.

The Council's inaction was suggested by Hammarskjold himself Aug. 21 in an address to the Council in which he defended his refusal to use UN troops to suppress the secessionist Katanga government, and warned that further opposition to UN action by the central Congolese government would force "reconsideration" of the UN's role in the country.

Hammarskjold agreed to set up an advisory committee of nations that had contributed UN contingents to assist him in carrying out his Congo mandate. He said he had received "the formal assurance of the Belgian government of completion of the withdrawal of all combat troops within at the most 8 days." Some technical, noncombat personnel temporarily were to remain at the Kamina and Kitona bases.

Hammarskjold, who said that he did not "ask for a confirmation by the Security Council of the obvious," declared that "it was made clear in my . . . statements and in those of a majority of the Council that, given the withdrawal of the Belgian troops from Katanga, the conflict between the central government and the provincial authorities was an internal matter." At no point in Council debate on its Aug. 9 resolution, he asserted, "did it emerge that United Nations troops . . . would be introduced in order to impose the authority of the central government on the rebellious provincial leaders."

Leopoldville Retracts Threats

Premier Lumumba aeclared in a statement issued in Leopoldville Aug. 22 that he was "satisfied" with the Security Council's latest debate on the Congo and had abandoned plans to oust UN troops and replace them with forces from friendly Asian and African nations. Lumumba based his satisfaction on the fact that Council members had not "blamed" the Congo government for its dispute with the UN and that the Congo's aims had been fulfilled when Hammarskjold "committed himself to get Belgian forces out of the Congo within a week."

Lumumba had accused Hammarskjold Aug. 19 of "blackmail" for threatening reconsideration of UN aid if Congolese attacks on UN personnel continued. He had declared that the Congo was "the property of no one" and was "ready to renounce the services" of the UN. He repeated demands for the "withdrawal of all white troops" from the UN Force and warned that if the Security Council ignored his demands for action against Katanga, he would call for African aid in marching into the secessionist province. Lumumba said he would not need Soviet support because "all African nations will heed our call."

At a series of Leopoldville news conferences Aug. 20, Lumumba withdrew his demands on condition that the UN rid itself of white officers who, he said, had worked with the Belgians. He urged, however, that a UN withdrawal from the Congo be carried out soon after the Belgian troops' departure because the UN's "white troops" hoped to "substitute United Nations colonialism for Belgian colonialism."

USSR Opposes UN Congo Program

The Soviet mission to the UN Aug. 20 denounced Hammarskjold's proposed Congo aid program as an attempt at "a new form of colonial enslavery of the Congolese people under the disguise of the United Nations flag." The statement, issued by Vasily Kuznetsov, charged that UN civil officials in the Congo had been drawn from "military-political groupings headed by the United States" and would act in the interests of the Western powers.

The Soviet government's opposition to Western and UN policies in the Congo had been made clear in these earlier statements:

A declaration issued July 31 by the USSR's Tass News agency accused NATO powers of having encouraged Belgium's intervention in the Congo and warned that the USSR would take "resolute measures to rebuff the aggressors" if Belgian troops were not withdrawn immediately.

Statements published in Pravda Aug. 3 accused Hammarskjold and UN Undersecy. Bunche of "pro-American" efforts to keep control of the Congo for the NATO "colonial powers." Pravda charged Aug. 13 that Hammarskjold had played a "disgraceful role" in the Congo by dealing with Katanga Pres. Tshombe and refusing to help the Congo government.

A statement issued Aug. 16 by Tass demanded that "troops of other countries" be sent to the Congo if UN forces failed to "cut short the occupation of Katanga" and arrest separatist leaders who were "at the bidding of foreign powers."

SEPARATIST MOVEMENTS FOUGHT

Lumumba Orders Offensive

Congolese government troops were sent into Kasai Province by Premier Lumumba Aug. 24 in an attempt to put down the secessionist movements threatening his regime.

A force of 200 soldiers was airlifted to Luluabourg, capital of Kasai, Aug. 24, and small mobile units of Congolese troops crossed the border from neighboring Leopoldville Province to begin occupying centers between the border and Luluabourg. 2 columns numbering an estimated 600 troops advanced from Luluabourg into southern Kasai Aug. 27, occupying the secessionist capital of Bakwanga and moving to within 20 miles of the Katanga provincial border Aug. 28. 10 Congolese soldiers were reported wounded Aug. 29 in fighting with secessionist forces and pro-secessionist Baluba tribesmen in the Bakwanga-Luputa area.

Katanga troops were flown Aug. 25 to Kaniama, on the provincial border with Kasai, to begin preparations against an attack by Lumumba's troops. Pres. Tshombe announced Aug. 28 that roads and bridges leading into Katanga from Kasai had been mined or blown up.

'Mining State' Collapses

The occupation of Kasai Province, ostensibly ordered to end fighting between Lulua and Baluba tribesmen in which hundreds had been reported killed, ended an independent "Mining State" proclaimed Aug. 9 by Albert Kalonji, Baluba leader and head of a rival group in the Congolese National Movement, whose dominant faction was led by Lumumba.

The short-lived Mining State occupied the diamond-rich area of Kasai surrounding Luluabourg and Bakwanga, the new state's capital. In a message dispatched to UN Secy. Gen. Hammarskjold Aug. 10, Kalonji announced that the new government had been established and asked that UN troops be sent to guard its borders. Kalonji was installed Aug. 23 as president of Mining State at the head of a 10-member cabinet. Kalonji and Tshombe Aug. 25 signed agreements federating Mining State and Katanga and pledging Katanga military aid against invasion.

Kalonji said at an Elisabethville news conference Aug. 27 that Mining State forces were regrouping and would continue to fight Congo army troops despite the capture of Bakwanga. But Tshombe criticized Kalonji Aug. 28 for fleeing from Lumumba's troops and made it clear that no Katangans would be sent to defend Mining State.

Dissidents Seek Federation

The secessionist movement, begun with Tshombe's proclamation of Katangan independence July 11, was supported by Kasai, Equator, Kivu and Leopoldville Province dissidents who joined with other opponents of the Lumumba regime to demand a loose federation of Congolese states.

Tshombe announced in Elisabethville July 16 that Kasai envoys sent by Kalonji and a Kivu delegation sent by Anicet Kashamura had arrived in Katanga with proposals to federate the 3 provinces. He said federation also had been urged by tribal leaders in the Ruanda-Urundi UN trusteeship territory. Tshombe issued a call July 17 for all Congo provinces to join Katanga in "a freely accepted federation . . . opposed to communism."

The Central Committee of the Abako Party, at a Leopoldville meeting presided over by Congolese Pres. Kasavubu, adopted Aug. 7 a political program calling for replacement of the Lumumba regime by a confederation of autonomous provincial states. In a message cabled to Secy. Gen. Hammarskjold the same day, Kasavubu asserted that the Lumumba government was incapable of restoring order in the Congo and that confederation was the only form of government acceptable to a majority of Congolese. Vice Premier Gaston Diomi of Leopoldville Province said Aug. 8 that he had cabled the UN to urge creation of a Congolese federation. He said his huge Mukongo tribe had "rejected" Lumumba's rule.

UN Troops Attacked

Congolese soldiers attacked and beat 8 Canadian soldiers of the UN Force at Leopoldville airport Aug. 18. The assault, the first of several such incidents, was attributed to the Lumumba government's encouragement of popular fears that white UN troops were Belgian agents seeking to reimpose colonial rule.

The Canadians, technicians boarding a plane for Luluabourg, were surrounded by armed Congolese, ordered to lie on the ground and were beaten with gun butts and robbed. Capt. J. C. Terchereau was clubbed into unconsciousness before Ghanaian UN troops arrived and rescued the men. All Congolese troops except a 6-man squad were cleared from the airport later that day by UN troops authorized to use force if necessary.

Lumumba, charging Aug. 21 that "spies and plotters" were being sent into the Congo through the neighboring (formerly French) Congo Republic, ordered all traffic and communications severed with Brazzaville, across the Congo River from Leopoldville. In a N.Y. Times interview the same day, Lumumba charged that there were "secret accords among the United States, France, Britain and Belgium for the uranium of Katanga" and a Western plot to separate Katanga from the Congo.

Congolese troops in Stanleyville, capital of Equator Province, attacked and clubbed 8 U.S. airmen at the city's airport and 3 UN Force officers at the local UN headquarters Aug. 27. The Americans, crewmen of an Air Force Globemaster carrying UN equipment, were injured severely before their rescue by Ethiopian UN troops.

An attempt to calm anti-white hysteria was made by Lumumba Aug. 28 in an address at a Stanleyville political rally. Lumumba said: "You must welcome white men who come to help us and work with us; you must take them into your huts and give them beer and bread"; many whites had helped the Congo in its "struggle for independence"; "you must never hate the Europeans, but only exploitation." (Lumumba also declared that the Congo could match the economic progress achieved by the U.S. and USSR. Asserting that 500,000 Congolese had been "deported as slaves" to America, he said: "Africans built America and developed America. They are the reason that America has become a great world power. If Africans could achieve that in the New World, they can achieve it in their own continent.")

Africans Back Both Lumumba, UN

Delegations from 13 African nations met in Leopoldville Aug. 25-31 in a Conference of Independent African States convoked by Lumumba to discuss African unity and to demonstrate African support for his government. The meeting, convened by Lumumba as nearby anti-government demonstrators were being dispersed by police gunfire, was attended by groups from the Cameroons, Ethiopia, Ghana, Guinea, Liberia, Libya, Morocco, Sudan, Togo, Tunisia, the UAR and the Algerian Provisional Government in Tunis.

Led by Tunisian Foreign Secy. Sadok Mokkadem, delegates were reported Aug. 31 to have warned Lumumba to halt Congolese resistance to UN Force operations or endanger African support for his government. Conference pressure forced Lumumba to pay homage to "the magnificent work" of the UN in the Congo in an address at the closing session Aug. 31. The resolutions approved by the conference (1) indorsed UN actions in the Congo, (2) expressed regret that "some incidents have troubled the collaboration and cooperation" between the UN and Congolese government, (3) condemned "secessionist and colonialist movements aimed at dividing the Congo" and (4) called for increased African aid to the Congo in coordination with the UN program.

BELGIAN FORCES LEAVE CONGO

Hammarskjold Obtains Withdrawal

UN Undersecy. Ralph Bunche announced in Leopoldville Aug. 29 that all Belgian combat troops, excluding technicians to be retained at Kamina and Kitona, would be withdrawn from the Congo "by dawn tomorrow" under terms of pledges obtained by Hammarskjold for completion of the withdrawal within a week.

Hammarskjold, however, disclosed Aug. 31 that he had protested to Belgian Rep.-to-UN Walter Loridan against Belgium's failure to carry out the promised withdrawal. The protest, made public in Hammarskjold's 3d report on the Congo to the Security Council, asked Belgium to withdraw its remaining combat troops "immediately." Hammarskjold's report made it clear that Belgian technicians would be permitted to remain at the Kamina and Kitona bases only to the extent they were required by the occupying UN Force contingents.

Hammarskjold charged Sept. 4 that 650 Belgian paratroops remained at Kitona and that all were combat, not specialist, troops. A Hammarskjold message Sept. 5 to the Belgian UN mission criticized the delay in the departure of paratroops from the Kamina base to Ruanda-Urundi and rejected Belgian explanations that some withdrawals had been held up by the failure of UN troops to relieve Belgians at their posts. Hammarskjold said the withdrawal of Belgian combat troops had not been conditional on their relief by the UN Force.

Completion of the removal of Belgian combat troops from the Congo was reported Sept. 9 in a message to Hammarskjold from J. De Thier, interim Belgian representative at the UN. The Belgian message said that troops remaining in the Kitona base area were technicians and airfield guards whose withdrawal would be conducted in agreement with UN Force contingents occupying the base.

(The exchanges of Belgian and UN messages on the troop withdrawal were made public at UN headquarters in New York Sept. 8 and 10. Included was a note in which Belgium explained that a shipment of arms made to Katanga Sept. 7 had been the fault of a minor official filling an order placed before June 30.)

(Rajeshwar Dayal, Indian high commissioner to Pakistan, was appointed by Hammarskjold Aug. 20 to replace Bunche as his personal representative in the Congo. Bunche left Leopoldville Aug. 30 and returned to New York to brief Hammarskjold and Dayal on the Congo situation.)

COUP AGAINST LUMUMBA FAILS

Kasavubu Leads Opposition

An attempt by Congolese Pres. Kasavubu to oust Premier Lumumba and replace his government with a cabinet headed by Senate Pres. Joseph Ileo was frustrated Sept. 5-6 by Lumumba with the support of police and troops in the Leopoldville area.

Kasavubu declared in a Leopoldville radio broadcast Sept. 5 that Lumumba had failed to restore order in the Congo and instead had "plunged the nation into fratricidal warfare." Acting under Congolese constitutional provisions empowering the president to remove a premier lacking confirmation by Parliament, Kasavubu removed Lumumba from office and named as his successor Ileo, a conservative known to favor a confederation of autonomous Congo provinces. Kasavubu called on the UN Force to assume responsibility for "peace and order" in the Congo.

Lumumba, broadcasting over Leopoldville radio 1½ hours later despite a UN order barring all unauthorized persons from the station, declared that "Kasavubu is no longer chief of state" and his removal of the government was invalid. Appealing to Congolese troops for support against Kasavubu, Lumumba said that "nobody, not even chief-of-state Kasavubu, has the right to revoke the government . . . elected by the people. . . ."

The UN Force occupied Leopoldville radio Sept. 6. A heavy cordon of UN troops surrounded UN headquarters in downtown Leopoldville and Kasavubu's home outside the city. UN units halted most Leopoldville traffic and urged civilians to stay at home, but did not attempt to take control of the city from Congolese forces. Congolese police fired on demonstrators in downtown Leopoldville Sept. 6 as they sought to march on Lumumba's home to demand he obey Kasavubu's orders. Several demonstrators, supporters of Kasavubu, Kasai secessionist Albert Kalonji and Equator Province secessionist Jean Bolikango, were reported killed or wounded before the clashes were ended.

(Bolikango, Kasavubu's rival for the presidency and a leader of the Bangalia tribe from which most Congolese army troops were drawn, was arrested Sept. 1 in Gmena, Equator Province on Lumumba's orders and was brought to Leopoldville. He was freed from a Leopoldville prison Sept. 7 by a raiding party of pro-Kasavubu troops.)

Parliament Backs Government

The Congolese National Assembly's members voted Sept. 7 by 60-19 to approve a motion declaring the reciprocal ousters of Lumumba and Kasavubu "null and nonexistent." The Assembly vote, a victory for Lumumba, came after Lumumba had accused Kasavubu of plotting with the UN and "imperialists" to end Congolese independence. Lumumba did not, however, demand a confidence vote or attempt to legitimatize his ouster of Kasavubu. The session was attended by 91 of the 137 Assembly deputies, but members of Kasavubu's Abako party walked out before the voting began.

The Congolese Senate voted by 41-2 Sept. 8 to express confidence in the Lumumba regime and to avoid Pres. Kasavubu's attempt to dismiss Lumumba and replace him with Ileo. The Senate vote came after Lumumba had appealed to it for support against UN and Belgian efforts to impose "slavery" on the Congo and had demanded that the UN Force relinquish its control of Leopoldville radio and the Congo's airports or withdraw from the country. Lumumba was opposed only by Foreign Min. Bomboko and Albert Delvaux, supporters of Kasavubu's effort to oust the government.

Lumumba announced Sept. 9 that he had assumed Kasavubu's functions as chief of state and had taken personal command of the Congo's armed forces. Lumumba also announced the dismissal from his cabinet of the 3 ministers who had backed Kasavubu's attempt to oust him: Bomboko, Delvaux and Finance Min. Pascal Nkayi.

In a communique issued later Sept. 9, Kasavubu reiterated his Sept. 5 dismissal of Lumumba and ordered Ileo to present a cabinet to Parliament. He declared

Parliament's votes backing Lumumba to be constitutionally void. Ileo told newsmen in Leopoldville Sept. 11 that he had begun political soundings with Congolese provincial leaders, including secessionists Moise Tshombe and Albert Kalonji, and was preparing to form a government. Ileo said he had named Bomboko foreign minister and head of a new Congo mission to the UN.

Lumumba was arrested Sept. 12 by Congolese troops on a warrant signed by Kasavubu. He was released after 3 hours, however, and staged a "victory" parade through downtown Leopoldville to the radio station, where UN troops refused to permit him to broadcast. Newsmen reported that Lumumba had been taken to Camp Leopold II, near the capital, but had been released by high army officers after he tricked them into accepting an invalid resignation from the premiership.

A joint session of Parliament voted by 88-25 Sept. 13 to grant Lumumba "special powers" to oppose Kasavubu's efforts to overthrow his regime. The Parliamentary vote was counted and announced by Lumumba supporters, who claimed the session was attended by at least 113 senators and deputies—2 more than a quorum. Newsmen expressed doubt, however, that more than 90 were present.

RUSSIAN INTERVENTION BLOCKED

UN Halts Red Planes

Acting on the orders of Secy. Gen. Hammarskjold, the UN Force seized control of the airports in Leopoldville, Stanleyville, Luluabourg and other cities Sept. 6 to prevent the transportation of Congolese troops in a fleet of Soviet aircraft put at the Lumumba government's disposal.

The Soviet planes, 10 to 15 Ilyushin-14 twin-engine civil transports, had been reported in use carrying Lumumba's troops to Stanleyville since Sept. 2. They began transporting Congolese troops into Kasai via the Luluabourg and Bakwanga airports Sept. 4-5, before the UN occupied and closed the Congo's airports to all but UN aircraft. The Soviet planes, said to bear Congolese civil markings and to be flown by civilian Russian crews, were supplemented by an estimated 100 Soviet trucks landed at the port of Matadi. The Soviet troop-carrying flights were said to have been effectively halted by the UN's closure of the airports.

Hammarskjold ordered the airport closure extended to Katanga Province Sept. 8 to halt any aggressive moves by Tshombe's forces and presumably to avert charges of UN favoritism in the struggle between Katanga and the central Congolese government. (The order apparently was unconnected with the reported arrival in Elisabethville Sept. 7 of a shipment of 9 tons of Belgian arms and munitions. The Belgian UN mission was warned by Hammarskjold Sept. 8 that he would protest the shipment, said to be the 4th delivered recently by Sabena airliners, if the Elisabethville reports were proven true.) The UN flight ban was violated only in Katanga, where Belgian light planes were reported in use Sept. 9.

The UN ended its control of Leopoldville radio and opened all Congo and Katanga airports to "peaceful traffic" Sept. 13. UN troops were ordered to remain in control of the airports to insure limitation of their use to non-military aircraft.

Africans, USSR Oppose UN Moves

3 African states participating in the UN Force—the UAR, Ghana and Guinea—withdrew or threatened to withdraw their troops from the force unless the UN gave up its control of Leopoldville radio and the Congo's airports. UAR Deputy Presidential Affairs Min. Abdel Kader Hatem announced in Cairo Sept. 12 that the 650-man UAR battalion in the Congo had been instructed to withdraw from the UN command and return home. He blamed the withdrawal on the UN's "flagrant violation of the Congo's sovereignty" by its takeover of the radio and airports. Ghanaian Pres. Kwame Nkrumah cabled Hammarskjold Sept. 13 to warn that Ghanaian troops would be withdrawn from the force and put at the orders of "the legitimate Lumumba government" unless the UN returned Leopold-

ville radio to Congolese control.

The Soviet government, in a note delivered to Hammarskjold and made public Sept. 10, demanded that UN troops return the Congo's airports and radio facilities to Congolese control. The Soviet message, sent in reply to a Hammarskjold note of Sept. 5, asserted that Soviet provision of "civil aircraft and trucks" to the Congo government did not violate the Security Council resolution on the Congo.

U.S. Warns Soviets On Arms Aid

Pres. Eisenhower declared Sept. 7 that the U.S. took a "most serious view" of the USSR's supply of aircraft and trucks to the Lumumba government. In a statement read at a Washington news conference, Mr. Eisenhower said: "The United States deplores the unilateral action of the Soviet Union in supplying aircraft and other equipment for military purposes to the Congo, . . . aggravating an already serious situation which finds Africans killing other Africans"; the UN's program of collective aid for the Congo was "threatened by the Soviet action, which seems to be motivated entirely by the Soviet Union's political designs in Africa."

The President conceded that inspection of the Soviet planes when they stopped near Athens en route to the Congo had shown them to be carrying legitimate cargo "for peaceful purposes." He said, however, that the planes would be used for military purposes by the Congolese government and that the Soviet action was a violation of the UN decision barring great-power military contingents from the Congo.

Truce With Dissidents Reported

The UN announced Sept. 10 that the Congolese army had agreed to a UN-supervised cease-fire in its campaign against secessionist forces in Kasai and Katanga Provinces. Col. S. M. Mollersware of Sweden was named to head a special 14-member UN truce supervisory commission to enforce the cease-fire on the Katanga-Kasai-

Kivu frontier. The UN truce team arrived in Elisabethville Sept. 12 to begin enforcing the cease-fire.

Despite the UN announcement, Lumumba told newsmen in Leopoldville Sept. 10 that his government had not ordered a cease-fire and that Congolese troops were continuing their "occupation" of Katanga. Congolese troops reportedly had crossed from Kivu Province into the Kongolo region of northern Katanga Sept. 8. The Congolese were said to have withdrawn in the next 2 days after they failed to get vehicles across the Luzka River on the border between Kivu and Katanga.

The withdrawal of all Congolese troops from Katanga and South Kasai was ordered Sept. 18 by the central government. 2 columns of Congolese troops that had penetrated Katanga in a pincer movement toward the northern town of Kongolo were reported to have left the province by Sept. 18. The first column, numbering 300 men, was discovered 25 miles west of Kongolo Sept. 15 by Mali UN troops. The 2d column, numbering 800, advanced through Kilubi to positions near Kongolo, but agreed to UN cease-fire proposals when faced by Katanga troops Sept. 17.

Secy. Gen. Hammarskjold warned Pres. Tshombe Sept. 21 that the 4,000 UN troops in Katanga had been ordered to use force if necessary to prevent the massacre of Baluba tribesmen by provincial troops and police. Hammarskjold's message to Tshombe marked the first public authorization of the use of force by UN troops in the Congo.

The warning was based on UN reports of the slaughter of 68 Balubas by Katanga provincial police Sept. 15-16 in Luena, a tin-mining center 250 miles north of Elisabethville. The Katanga Balubas, enemies of Tshombe's Lunda tribe, were said to have killed 2 persons in an attack on Tshombe supporters in Luena Sept. 13. 125 Katanga provincial police arrived in Luena Sept. 15 and reportedly began random shooting of Balubas in sight of an Ethiopian UN contingent based in the town. The Luena incident was described by Katanga officials as one of several police actions made necessary by a Baluba tribal revolt. (An estimated 1/3 of Katanga's 1.5 million inhabitants were Balubas.) 35 Balubas were reported to have been killed in attacks on provincial police in Manono Sept. 13-14.

Irish UN troops protected the police and 73 marooned Belgians until their evacuation. A local chief and 3 of his sons were reported killed Sept. 15 in Bukama by Balubas.

UN BACKS HAMMARSKJOLD POLICIES

An emergency special session of the UN General Assembly, convened in New York 3 days before the opening of the Assembly's regular 15th annual meeting, declared its support Sept. 20 for Secy. Gen. Hammarskjold's policies in the Congo. The emergency special session, 4th in the history of the UN (others: Suez and Hungary in 1956, Lebanon in 1958), was summoned by the Security Council after the USSR had cast its 90th veto Sept. 17 to block a Tunisian-Ceylonese resolution backing Hammarskjold.

Security Council Action

The Security Council session was requested Sept. 7 by Hammarskjold in order to (1) seek further clarification of his mandate to act in the Congo, and (2) make clear the Council's disapproval of the USSR's provision of planes and military material for the Lumumba government's war against secessionism. Hammarskjold's Sept. 7 report to the Council warned that the UN Force, thus far neutral in the Congo's internal power struggle, might be forced to disarm Congolese "military units which . . . are an obstacle to the reestablishment of law and order." He warned that the aid given Lumumba's faction "from the outside" had made the Congolese crisis "increasingly grave," and must be stopped.

The Council was convened Sept. 9 by Egidio Ortona of Italy, its president for September. It immediately rejected a Soviet proposal that it move the session to Leopoldville "to acquaint itself with the situation in the Congo." The Soviet proposal, rejected by a vote of 6-3 (USSR, Poland and Ceylon in favor, 2 abstentions), was made by First Deputy Foreign Min. Kuznetsov on the basis of a Sept. 8 request by Premier Lumumba that Council members come to Leopoldville to "see for themselves the situation existing . . . as a result of the United Nations' interference in the Congo's domestic problems."

The Council adjourned temporarily Sept. 10 after receiving Congolese government requests that it delay debate to permit a Congolese delegation to come to New York and after being informed that Pres. Kasavubu had formed a government replacing the Lumumba regime. The Council took no action on a renewed demand by Kuznetsov that it order Hammarskjold to withdraw the UN Force from the Congo's radio stations and airports. A Soviet demand that the Council reconvene immediately to debate the alleged "sabotage" of its orders by Hammarskjold was ignored Sept. 13.

The Council reconvened Sept. 14 and refused to seat either of 2 rival Congolese delegations sent to New York for the session. A Soviet proposal to seat a Lumumba delegation headed by Thomas Kanza was defeated with 3 votes in favor and 8 abstentions. No vote was taken on seating the 2d delegation, representing Kasavubu and headed by Justin Bomboko.

Soviet Rep.-to-UN Valerian A. Zorin, in an unprecedented attack on Hammarskjold, charged Sept. 14 that he had been a "willing tool" of Western colonialists in the Congo and had "taken under his trusteeship the stooges of Belgian aggression." Zorin accused Hammarskjold of "an abuse of power granted to him by the Security Council." Zorin said 20,000 Belgian troops remained in the Congo, many of them in the guise of technicians.

2 conflicting draft resolutions on the Congo were introduced in the Council Sept. 15 by U.S. Amb-to-UN James J.Wadsworth and Zorin: (1) the U.S. resolution called on Hammarskjold to continue his "vigorous" implementation of Council decisions. It urged contributions to a UN fund for the Congo to be controlled by Hammarskjold. It urged negotiation of Congolese factions' differences and asked all nations to refrain from unilateral aid to any Congo factions. It concluded with a reaffirmation of the UN Force's mandate. (2) The Soviet resolution demanded that Hammarskjold and the UN command "put an end to all forms of interference in the internal affairs of the . . . Congo" and withdraw UN guards from airports and radio stations. It demanded dismissal of the UN command for "gross vio-

lations" of Council orders and appealed for donations of economic aid directly to the Congolese government.

A compromise resolution intended to break the U.S.-Soviet deadlock was presented to the Council Sept. 16 by Tunisian Foreign Min. Mongi Slim and Sir Claude Corea of Ceylon. The compromise contained most major provisions of the U.S. resolution—indorsement of Hammarskjold's actions, continuation of the UN Force's mandate, appeals against unilateral military aid for the Congo and for a UN-supervised Congo aid fund—but it asked that aid be administered in consultation with the Congolese government and that no action be taken that would "undermine the territorial integrity and the political independence" of the Congo.

The USSR's 90th veto in the Security Council was cast by Zorin Sept. 17 to prevent adoption of the Tunisian-Ceylonese resolution.

General Assembly Action

An emergency special session of the General Assembly was summoned Sept. 17 at the request of the U.S. under the 1950 Uniting for Peace Resolution (permitting international problems to be brought before the Assembly in case of a prior deadlock in the Security Council). Summoning of the emergency session was approved in the Security Council by a vote of 8-2 (USSR and Poland opposed, France abstaining).

In a surprise move at the first meeting of the emergency session later Sept. 17, U.S. delegate Wadsworth asked that the Assembly immediately vote to admit 14 new African states to UN membership. Wadsworth contended that "the fate of the Congo is of extraordinary and vital importance to the rest of Africa, and the United States believes those most directly concerned should be permitted to participate in the debate." the U.S. proposal, opposed by Zorin, was supported the same day by a vote of 43-0 (26 abstentions, 13 absent) but failed to win a required 2/3 Assembly majority.

Addressing the Assembly Sept. 18, Hammarskjold denied Soviet charges that he had mismanaged the UN mission in the Congo and had disobeyed Security Council orders. Hammarskjold contended that he had been forced, by the "de facto" situation in Katanga and the Council's refusal to sanction the use of force, to negotiate with Katanga Pres. Tshombe on UN Force entry into the province. He said that the UN's consultation with the central Congolese government had been "of an unusual intensity" despite "great difficulties." Reaffirming his rejection of Lumumba's demands that the UN troops restore the central government's authority in Katanga, he asserted that "no . . . government as an act of sovereignty can turn a United Nations force into a national force which it uses for its own purposes."

Hammarskjold's role in the Congo was supported by a draft resolution introduced in the Assembly Sept. 19 by Alex Quaison-Sackey of Ghana with the co-sponsorship of 16 Asian and African nations. The Afro-Asian resolution, similar to the Tunisian-Ceylonese draft vetoed in the Security Council, called for (1) Hammarskjold's continued "vigorous action" to carry out Council orders and to assist "the central government of the Congo in the restoration . . . of law and order . . . and to safeguard its unity, territorial integrity and political independence"; (2) appointment of a UN conciliation group to aid negotiations among conflicting Congolese factions; (3) contributions to a UN fund to be used under UN control in consultation with the Congo government; (4) "all states to refrain from the . . . provision of arms . . . military personnel and other assistance for military purposes . . . " except at Hammarskjold's request.

A Soviet resolution, presented to the Assembly later Sept. 19 by Zorin, embodied the USSR's opposition to Hammarskjold's actions in the Congo. It called for: condemnation of Belgium for "armed aggression" against the Congo with NATO support; the withdrawal of all NATO (Belgian) troops from the Congo; restraint of actions that would undermine the Congo's integrity and independence.

The Assembly voted Sept. 20 by 70-0 (USSR and Soviet bloc, France and South Africa abstaining, Bolivia absent) to approve the Asian-African resolution supporting Hammarskjold. The key section calling for cessation of foreign military aid to the Congo was approved by 80-0, with the

USSR voting in favor. Zorin did not ask Assembly action on the Soviet resolution or on several amendments to the Asian-African resolution proposed late Sept. 19 in an effort to weaken the draft's support of Hammarskjold.

LUMUMBA REGIME DEPOSED

Mobutu Leads Army Coup

The Lumumba government was ousted from office Sept. 14 by a military coup led by Col. Joseph D. Mobutu, 29, Congolese Army chief of staff. In a broadcast announcing the coup, Mobutu declared that the army would assume direction of the government until the beginning of 1961 but that Lumumba and Kasavubu would retain their current posts. He asserted that the army move was not a coup d'etat, but was a "simple, peaceful revolution" to "neutralize" the strife-ridden Congolese government. He said the army had been forced to act by the chaos resulting from the struggle for power between Lumumba and Kasavubu. He appealed for UN and foreign support of the army effort to restore order. Mobutu was said to control 3,000 to 4,000 troops in the Leopoldville area.

Senate Pres. Joseph Ileo, who had been designated premier during Kasavubu's unsuccessful attempt to oust Lumumba, declared his backing of the army coup Sept. 14 as the only way to end the Congo crisis. Ileo dismissed Gen. Lundula as army commander and named Mobutu, a former soldier and journalist, to replace him. Decrees signed by Ileo and Pres. Kasavubu suspended Parliament for 2 months. They were enforced by Mobutu's troops, who dispersed an attempted Senate meeting Sept. 15 and occupied Parliament Sept. 16.

Lumumba was arrested on Mobutu's orders Sept. 14 and was taken to Camp Leopold II by military police. He was escorted to his Leopoldville home the next day by UN and Congolese troops loyal to Mobutu after he had only narrowly escaped lynching in the camp by Congolese soldiers from Kasai Baluba tribes that had been decimated by Lumumba's invasion force. Mobutu's troops arrested most members of Lumumba's personal staff in Leopoldville Sept.

16. Lumumba escaped from his guarded home Sept. 16. He returned Sept. 18 and told newsmen he would have Mobutu arrested and would call a new session of Parliament, but he disappeared again later Sept. 18 for 2 days.

Notes to the Soviet and Czech embassies in Leopoldville Sept. 16 from Kasavubu and Ileo ordered all Soviet-bloc diplomats, technicians and other personnel to leave the Congo within 48 hours. Mobutu, in his initial announcement of the army coup, had warned Sept. 14 that the army wanted all Russian, Czech and "other Socialist" personnel expelled from the country. Soviet Amb. Mikhail D. Yakovlev and Czech Amb. Josef Virius left Leopoldville by plane Sept. 17, accompanied by nearly 100 staff members. Soviet-bloc embassy staffs and technicians in the Congo had been estimated at 450 persons. 11 of the Soviet transport planes lent to the Lumumba government landed in Cairo Sept. 20 on their way back to the USSR.

'Collegial' Government Formed

A 15-member nonpolitical caretaker regime chosen by Pres. Kasavubu was installed Sept. 20 by Col. Mobutu to administer the government until settlement of the Congo's political struggle. The interim regime, known as the College of High Commissioners, was headed by Justin Bomboko as president and high commissioner for foreign affairs. Other members were mainly young Congolese university students and graduates, among them Albert Ndele, vice president and high commissioner for financial affairs. Mobutu said Sept. 20 that the high commissioners would "conduct the general policy" of the Congo and "assume representation of the republic abroad." He said that neither the Lumumba nor the Ileo cabinets were entitled to exercise governmental authority; this was, he said, solely the function of the new high commissioners.

Lumumba, at a news conference at his Leopoldville home Sept. 20, denounced the "student government" as illegal and insisted that he remained the Congo's legal premier. He distributed copies of an "agreement of conciliation" in which, he said, Kasavubu had agreed to end their differences and back his cabinet. But Mobutu's troops ousted

Lumumba appointees from governmental offices Sept. 20, and expulsion orders were issued Sept. 21 for Lumumba's principal advisers, Serge Michel, a Frenchman, and Mme. Andree Blouin, who had a Guinean passport.

The high commissioners occupied Congo government offices Sept. 21 and announced plans for a public works program designed to reduce African unemployment, estimated at 80,000 in the Leopoldville area. They also reiterated cease-fire appeals to forces of Albert Kalonji in Kasai.

Congolese troops in Leopoldville mutinied against Mobutu Sept. 22 to protest reports of an increase in officers' pay, but they were dispersed by Congolese military police. Antoine Gizenga and Maurice Mpolo, respectively vice premier and sports minister in Lumumba's cabinet, were arrested Sept. 23 after an unsuccessful attempt to start a new revolt against Mobutu. Gizenga, Mpolo and Maj. Vital Jakasa were released the next day, reportedly on the intervention of Moroccan UN troops.

African Interference Charged

Col. Mobutu disclosed Sept. 21 that he had requested the withdrawal of Ghanaian and Guinean contingents of the UN Force because they had "interfered in internal affairs of the Congo." Mobutu reportedly charged that "Communists, Guineans and Pres. . . . Nkrumah of Ghana" had conspired to interfere in Congolese affairs. Mobutu's request was ignored by UN Force commanders on the ground that only Secy. Gen. Hammarskjold could determine the composition of the force.

Mobutu's charges of the intervention apparently were founded on the efforts of 5 African nations—Ghana, Guinea, Morocco, Sudan and the UAR—to conciliate between Lumumba and Kasavubu. Leopoldville envoys of the 5 states with Lumumba and Kasavubu Sept. 22-24, reportedly in an attempt to persuade Kasavubu to retain Lumumba as premier. In an apparent concession to the African states' pressure, Mobutu met with Lumumba Sept. 24 and said that if necessary he would "impose a conciliation." The efforts to bring the 2 leaders together apparently foundered on Lumumba's refusal to accept any restriction of his powers.

UN Operational Report

In his first report to Hammarskjold since becoming his personal representative in the Congo, Rajeshwar Dayal warned Sept. 26 that the Congo faced chaos, disease and disintegration unless its political leaders ended factional strife in the interests of preserving an independent and viable state. Dayal asserted that there was still "time for the Congolese leaders and people . . . to put an end to factional party strife . . . and to embark on the path of national unity." Continued division, he warned, would lead to "disorder and disintegration, dangerous . . . to the Congolese people," Africa and the entire world.

Dayal blamed the Congo crisis on an "almost complete lack of trained civil servants, executives and professional people of Congolese origin," which was made still worse by "a complete failure to arrange for any organized handover to the Congolese of the administrative machinery . . . or of essential public services." To this was added the "confusion, fear and disorder which gripped the country," the destruction of much essential equipment and the removal from the country of business funds. Under these conditions, Dayal reported, the UN Force, "thinly deployed . . . and circumscribed by its mandate, used its best efforts to safeguard lives, to prevent massacre and genocide," and succeeded in restoring order and halting fighting on the Katanga-Kasai frontier. UN civilian operations, Dayal said, had maintained essential food supplies, distributed from Leopoldville, and had partially restored essential public services, including transport and health.

Dayal reported that 16,382 troops had been supplied to the UN Force by 27 countries and that 16,220 men had been deployed to UN posts. An additional 2,437 men were expected and would raise the Force's personnel to 18,819. The following military contingents had been made available to the UN Force by Sept. 26: Argentina 10; Brazil 9; Burma 9; Canada 260; Ceylon 9; Denmark 30; Ethiopia 2,572; Ghana 2,291; Guinea 749; India 373; Indonesia 8; Ireland 1,383; Italy 90; Liberia 234; Malaya 8; Mali 577; Morocco 3,257; Netherlands 6; New Zealand 1; Norway 46; Pakistan 248; Sudan 398; Sweden 616; Switzerland 22; Tunisia 2,633; UAR

519; Yugoslavia 20. (An additional 144 civilian technicians and administrators staffed the UN civilian operation headed in the Congo by Sture C. Linner of Sweden. Emergency Red Cross medical teams from 19 countries were operating in the Congo under World Health Organization supervision. A drive was under way to recruit 400 doctors to man the Congo's 400 hospitals and medical centers, all but 50 of which were without physicians.)

MOBUTU GROUP TIGHTENS RULE

Kasavubu Gives Powers

All "executive and administrative authority" formally was turned over by Pres. Kasavubu Sept. 29 to the College of High Commissioners. Kasavubu, introducing the high commissioners to foreign diplomats at his Leopoldville home, said that Premier-designate Ileo's cabinet would permit the commissioners to exercise their functions until the restoration of "normal conditions" in the Congo. Kasavubu, who indorsed Mobutu's efforts to save the Congo from an "explosive situation," called on the UN and foreign nations to deal exclusively with the interim High Commission regime. The meeting was attended by 17 envoys representing the U.S. and most European nations, but was boycotted by Ghana, Guinea, Morocco and the UAR.

A round-table conference of leaders of all Congolese factions was proposed Sept. 27 by Mobutu to help settle the Lumumba-Kasavubu dispute. Mobutu asserted that the meeting had been approved by Kasavubu, Ileo, Lumumba and Katanga Pres. Tshombe. In conflicting statements issued after Mobutu's announcement, both Kasavubu and Lumumba claimed to have proposed the conference, and each said he would preside over it. But Tshombe, Jean Bolikango of Equator Province and Albert Kalonji of Kasai Province made clear Sept. 30-Oct. 1 that they would not attend if Lumumba presided.

(Documentary evidence that the Lumumba government had appealed to the USSR and Communist China for military aid and personnel was released Sept. 28 by the High Commission. Photocopies were made public of purported aid appeals signed by Lumumba and Deputy Premier Gizenga. The Gizenga message asked Communist China to give the Congo "personnel," tanks, planes, food and funds "immediately in order to . . . assure the integrity of its dangerously threatened territory." A copy of the Chinese reply made public Sept. 30 by Mobutu said that military personnel could not be provided "because of the vast distance and the present confused situation in the Congo." The Chinese letter, allegedly signed by Chou En-lai, offered the Lumumba regime $2 1/2 million in aid and pledged to study its request for arms. The interim government also made public Sept. 28 purported copies of a letter in which Ghana Pres. Nkrumah advised Lumumba to bide his time and feign cooperation with the UN and Kasavubu in order to use them and later oust them. The Ghana letter, dated Sept. 12, advised Lumumba to work with his "closest enemies" and to consult Nkrumah when "in doubt.")

UN Prevents Lumumba Arrest

The UN command in the Congo refused Oct. 11 to permit the arrest of Premier Lumumba by troops of Mobutu and the High Commission government.

An ultimatum issued Oct. 10 by High Commission Pres. Bomboko gave the UN command 24 hours to honor a warrant for Lumumba's arrest or face armed action by the Congolese Army. The ultimatum said UN troops guarding Lumumba had refused to accept the arrest warrant; it warned that "if the population has to combat the United Nations" to enforce High Commission orders, "it will do so." The UN command, in a statement issued Oct. 11 after a meeting between Bomboko, Mobutu and Rajeshwar Dayal, refused to turn over Lumumba to Mobutu on grounds that the ultimatum was an appeal to "political violence" and that Lumumba possessed Parliamentary immunity against arrest. It noted that the Congo's "principal political dignitaries . . . have long enjoyed the protection of a United Nations guard" and that the UN could not relax the guard to permit service of an "invalid" arrest warrant.

The ultimatum for Lumumba's arrest was issued after Lumumba had toured Leopoldville with a UN Force escort

Oct. 9 to exhort African crowds to restore his power over the Congo. Lumumba had announced Oct. 7 a new cabinet that included Albert Kalonji and Jean Bolikango.

Katanga Accord Reported

Mobutu flew to Elisabethville Oct. 16 for talks with Katanga Pres. Tshombe. He announced in Leopoldville the next day that he had been pledged Tshombe's "moral, economic and financial backing" in his efforts to end the Congo crisis. Mobutu said he and Tshombe had reached agreement that (1) Katanga would remain in a Congo state based on "unity in diversity," (2) the interim High Commission would remain in office, (3) Lumumba, Kasavubu and the Congo Parliament would remain "neutralized" and (4) Tshombe would participate in a round-table conference of Congolese political leaders.

Lumumba Regime Dissolved

The High Commission announced Oct. 25 that Pres. Kasavubu had signed a constitutional decree legalizing the interim government under Col. Mobutu. Marcel Lihau, high commissioner for justice, declared to newsmen that the decree gave legal sanction to the removal of the Lumumba regime. He called on the UN to recognize the High Commission or face World Court action. The High Commission accused "a group of Asian-African states, spearheaded by Ghana, Guinea and Morocco," of plotting with UN officials to seize Leopoldville radio, disarm Mobutu's troops and reconvene the Congolese Parliament, presumably to restore Lumumba.

Mobutu and High Commission Pres. Bomboko agreed in a meeting Oct. 26 with Dayal and UN Force commanders to withdraw all Congolese troops from Leopoldville and confine them to barracks until they submitted to military discipline. UN troops were to assume "increased responsibility" for maintaining order in Leopoldville together with Congolese police.

The High Commission's hold on Leopoldville was reported to have weakened beginning Oct. 20, when Congolese troops again rioted and threatened the city's security. Pres. Cleophas Kamitatu of Leopoldville Province, a Lumumba supporter, charged Oct. 20 that Mobutu's troops were causing increasing disorders in the capital and surrounding areas. He threatened the province's secession unless Mobutu restored army discipline. 350 UN troops reinforced Kamitatu's provincial police Oct. 20 to help restore order. It was reported in Leopoldville dispatches Oct. 22-23 that Mobutu's control over his troops virtually had ended. Mobutu named Lt. Col. Louis Boboso, commander of an armored brigade in Thysville, to replace him during his absence and left Leopoldville Oct. 23 on an "inspection visit" to Coquilhatville. Drunken Congolese troops terrorized the African quarter of Leopoldville Oct. 23-24, halted cars and buses and beat their occupants and bystanders. 10 Bayaka tribesmen and a soldier were reported killed Oct. 22-23 in a clash 10 miles from the capital. The army disorders were accompanied by arrests of Lumumba supporters, presumably to forestall a new Lumumba effort to depose Mobutu and the High Commission government backed by his troops.

UN Against Belgians' Return

A reported influx into the Congo of numbers of Belgian civil servants, technicians and military advisers was assailed by Secy. Gen. Hammarskjold in notes to the Belgian and Katanga governments. The notes were rejected publicly Oct. 26-27 by Belgian Foreign Min. Pierre Wigny and Katanga Pres. Tshombe.

Hammarskjold's note to Belgium, delivered the previous week, demanded the recall of all Belgian "military, paramilitary and civilian" personnel from the Congo and urged that all future Belgian aid to the Congo be channeled through the UN. Wigny said at a Brussels UN Day meeting Oct. 26 that the note was devoid of meaning and would be rejected by his government. The message to Tshombe blamed continued tension in the Congo and Katanga on the continued presence of a "considerable" number of Belgians. It said the UN intended to "isolate the Belgian factor and eliminate it." Tshombe announced Oct. 27 that he had rejected this warning as "interference" in Katanga's affairs.

(The UN command in the Congo Oct. 31 rejected Tshombe's demands for the removal from Katanga of Ian Berendsen, UN representative in Elisabethville, and Col. Henry Byrnes of Ireland, UN military commander in northern Katanga. The UN command said the UN had not recognized the existence of a sovereign Katanga government and did not intend to submit its personnel to accreditation by the Tshombe regime.)

Dayal Assails Mobutu Rule

Rajeshwar Dayal asserted in a report to the UN General Assembly Nov. 3 that conditions in the Congo had "markedly deteriorated" due to the incompetence of the Mobutu regime and the growing intervention of returning Belgian colonial officials. The report said that "at the heart of the present confusion and disintegration in the Congo is the complete lack of progress in the way of a political settlement" among contenders who had reached a "complete stalemate." It said the only hope for creation of an effective Congo government lay in the restoration of the power of Pres. Kasavubu and the Congo Parliament.

Dayal, who returned to New York Nov. 4 to meet with Hammarskjold's Congo advisory committee, warned that "the single most disturbing . . . development . . . has been a steady and often rapid breakdown of law and order" due primarily to the "indiscipline" and "illegal and arbitrary acts" of the Congolese army. The failure to restore governmental authority was blamed by Dayal on the High Commission. As a result of "their inexperience, their lack of method and order, their susceptibility to outside [Belgian] influences," "the chaotic administrative . . . situation [had] reached the verge of collapse," Dayal said. Dayal expressed concern at the "return of Belgian nationals into many phases of public life in the Congo." He charged that many of them apparently had been recruited by Belgium to arm and lead "separatist Congolese forces." He asserted that the returnees were crippling UN operations and preventing a "return to constitutional government."

Belgians Denounce UN for 'Failure'

A statement issued in Brussels by Foreign Ministry spokesman Hans Taelemans Nov. 4 denounced Dayal's report as "unacceptable" and an effort to divert from Hammarskjold the blame for the UN's "failure" in the Congo. Belgium rejected any UN attempt to judge the motives for Belgian aid to the Congo or to force the withdrawal of Belgian technicians. A U.S. State Department statement Nov. 4 expressed "every confidence in the good faith of Belgium in its desire to be of assistance in the Congo." It cited sections of the report in which Belgian technicians' efforts were lauded as of "benefit to the country" and rejected "the implication to the contrary" contained elsewhere in the document.

Belgian Foreign Min. Wigny Nov. 14 assailed UN operations in the Congo as a "failure" and warned that Belgium would quit the world organization unless UN officials in the Congo were ordered to abide by "the protocol of public officials." Addressing a UN press conference, Wigny rejected the Dayal report and demands by Secy. Gen. Hammarskjold for withdrawal from the Congo of all Belgian officials and technicians. Wigny termed the Hammarskjold demands "stupid even for the United Nations" and insisted that the estimated 2,100 Belgians in the Congo had been sent there not by Belgium but by the central and provincial Congolese governments.

A U.S. delegation statement issued at the UN the next day rejected Wigny's contentions and said: "In our judgement, our joint effort in the Congo is by no means a failure"; Belgian cooperation with the UN would "benefit . . . all the people of the Congo"; the U.S. would continue to support the UN's efforts to "get on with the task" of restoring peace and order in the Congo.

UN Soldiers Die in Ambush

8 soldiers of the Irish contingent of the UN Force were killed Nov. 8 when tribesmen ambushed an 11-man UN patrol near Niemba on the Nyunzu-Albertville highway in northern Katanga. A 9th member of the patrol was missing.

The soldiers were members of the Irish 33d Battalion, based in Albertville and responsible for patrolling the truce zones created by the UN in Baluba tribal areas of northern Katanga. The attacking tribesmen were believed to be Balubas. In its first account of the ambush, reported Nov. 9, the UN command erroneously had reported that 10 Irish troops were killed.

KASAVUBU MISSION TO UN

Recognition Sought for New Regime

Congolese Pres. Kasavubu flew to New York Nov. 7 on what he said was a mission to "defend the sovereignty and independence of my country" before the UN Assembly and to protest attempts "to impose on us a neo-colonialism that is humiliating and unbearable." Kasavubu's voyage was said to have 3 specific objectives: (1) to prevent the return to power of Premier Lumumba; (2) to prevent UN dispatch of a Congo conciliation team to seek restoration of the Congo Parliament, in which Lumumba reportedly retained majority support; (3) to win UN recognition for the Congolese delegation sent to New York by Kasavubu and High Commission Pres. Bomboko.

Kasavubu addressed the UN Assembly Nov. 8 after it had adjourned its Congo debate the previous day to await his appearance. In a brief speech that avoided criticism of Hammarskjold or of UN operations in the Congo, Kasavubu informed the Assembly that he had assumed personal leadership of his delegation to the UN.

The Kasavubu speech was attacked in the Assembly Nov. 8 by Soviet Rep.-to-UN Zorin and by Ismail Toure of Guinea, one of 8 Asian-African states that had submitted a resolution Oct. 28 calling for recognition of the rival Congolese delegation sent to New York by Lumumba's government. The 8 Asian-African states, supported by the Soviet bloc, won an indefinite adjournment of the Assembly's Congo debate Nov. 9 to prevent the seating of Kasavubu's delegation. The motion for postponement was presented by Ghana with Guinean and Nigerian co-sponsorship and was adopted Nov. 9 by a 48-30 Assembly vote (USSR and Soviet bloc in favor). The U.S. delegation failed in efforts to win a temporary suspension of the debate.

The campaign for seating of the Kasavubu delegation was carried to the Assembly's Credentials Committee, which voted Nov. 10 to recommend that the delegation be accepted as the Congo's legal representatives. The vote was 6 to 1, with the USSR opposed and the UAR and Morocco absent. The Committee acted despite Zorin's charges that the U.S. was trying to "railroad" the UN into recognition of a regime opposed by a majority of the Congolese people.

UN supervision of a Congolese constitutional referendum on direct election of a president to replace Kasavubu was requested by Lumumba in a letter transmitted to Assembly Pres. Frederick Boland Nov. 14. Lumumba charged that Kasavubu was responsible for "anarchy and dictatorship" in the Congo and a "reign of terror" in Leopoldville. He said direct popular election of a new president was "the one and only way of restoring immediate peace and order to the Congo."

Kasavubu informed the UN Nov. 15 that Hammarskjold's plan to send a 15-nation conciliation group to the Congo was unacceptable. In a letter replying to UN notification that the conciliation group hoped to meet with him in Leopoldville, Kasavubu contended that the UN Charter contained no provisions permitting dispatch of a UN conciliation mission without specific agreement of the country concerned. He expressed doubt that the conciliation group would be successful and made it clear that he would not sanction its work, especially since some of its members (Ghana and Guinea) had taken "public positions on the internal politics of the Congo."

(The conciliation group had been formed Oct. 29 by Hammarskjold's Advisory Committee on the Congo, made up of all nations that had contributed troops to the UN Force. The conciliation group contained all members of the advisory committee except Sweden, Ireland and Canada. The group met Nov. 17, elected Jaja Wachuku of Nigeria as its chairman and fixed Nov. 26 as the date of its first working session in Leopoldville. But Hammarskjold delayed the group's departure Nov. 22 to make a new effort to win Kasavubu's agreement to its mission.)

Kasavubu Delegation Seated

The General Assembly voted Nov. 22 by 53 to 24 (19 abstentions) to seat the Kasavubu delegation rather than the envoys sent to UN headquarters by Lumumba. The Assembly vote implied the UN's recognition of the High Commission government dominated by Kasavubu and Col. Mobutu.

The seating of the Kasavubu delegation was supported by the U.S., most Western and Latin nations and by nearly all African states of the French Community. It was opposed by the USSR and Soviet bloc, India, Morocco, the UAR, Ghana, Guinea, Togo and other states that favored Lumumba's return to power. Abstentions were recorded by the Central African Republic, Ethiopia, Liberia, Libya, Somalia, Sudan and Tunisia. Nigeria and Upper Volta were absent. The vote to seat Kasavubu was the 3d in a series of key Assembly ballots on Congo representation. The Assembly had voted earlier Nov. 22 by 50 to 34 (13 abstentions) to reject a joint Ghanaian-Yugoslav-Indian resolution to adjourn the debate. It had rejected, by 51-36 vote (11 abstentions) Nov. 18, a Ghanaian motion to postpone the debate pending the projected visit to Leopoldville of the Congo conciliation committee.

Kasavubu left for Leopoldville Nov. 24 without agreeing to Hammarskjold's plans to send the conciliation mission to the Congo. At a meeting with Hammarskjold and Chrmn. Wachuku of the conciliation committee before his departure, Kasavubu reportedly warned that committee members' safety could not be assured if they went to Leopoldville without his permission. Hammarskjold had delayed the committee's departure for the 2d time Nov. 23 after Kasavubu indicated that he might agree to meet with the committee if it were expanded to include representatives of Ireland, Sweden and Canada.

UN Financial Crisis Reported

Secy. Gen. Hammarskjold warned the General Assembly's Administrative and Budgetary Committee Nov. 21 that the UN treasury was "virtually empty" and that the international force would have to be withdrawn from the Congo unless the UN received at least $20 million in new funds by Dec. 31. Hammarskjold said that at current spending rates the UN would be insolvent in a few months.

A report made public by Hammarskjold Oct. 25 had estimated that the UN Force in the Congo would cost $66,625,000 in 1960. Of this amount, the U.S. had contributed $5 million and a substantial amount of free services, Britain had pledged $2 million and Canada $1 million. More than $31 million in regular UN assessments, nearly ½ the UN's annual budget, remained unpaid, and Hammarskjold reported that only $12.5 million had been pledged for the proposed $100 million UN Congo Fund. The full cost of the first year of UN operations in the Congo was expected to reach $150-$200 million.

The Soviet bloc's refusal to contribute to the cost of UN operations in the Congo was made clear Oct. 21 by Miroslav Nacvalac of Czechoslovakia. Nacvalac told the Administrative and Budgetary Committee that the UN had played a "dirty role" in the Congo and that the Soviet bloc could not be expected to finance "the imperialist conspiracy in the Congo."

A U.S. offer to pay nearly ½ the cost of UN Congo operations in 1960 was presented to the General Assembly's Economic and Financial Committee Nov. 29 by Sen. George D. Aiken (R., Vt.), a member of the U.S. delegation. Aiken disclosed that the U.S. was ready to pay more than $30 million of the estimated $65 million spent for UN Congo operations, on the following basis: (1) payment of the $16,225,000 assessment assigned the U.S. as its regular 32.5% share of the Congo expenditures; (2) waiver of $10,317,621 of the $14 million owed the U.S. for transport and supplies for the Congo; (3) a cash contribution of $3.5-$4 million to reduce the Congo levies on poorer nations. Soviet Rep.-to-UN A. A. Roschin Nov. 29 reiterated to the committee the USSR's refusal to pay its Congo assessment. He demanded that Hammarskjold dissolve the international force to save the UN from bankruptcy. Roschin declared that UN funds had been spent in the Congo without proper authorization and that the countries responsible for the crisis there should be made to pay for it.

Ghanaian Ousted After Shooting

6 Congolese soldiers, among them Col. Joseph N'Kokolo, commander of the Congo Army's Leopoldville garrison, were killed in fighting that broke out in Leopoldville Nov. 21 when Tunisian troops of the UN Force apparently opened fire on the Congolese as they sought to seize Nathaniel A. Welbeck, Ghanaian envoy in Leopoldville, to expel him from the Congo. 2 Tunisians were killed in the clash.

Welbeck had been ordered to leave the Congo Nov. 18 by the Mobutu regime, but had refused on the ground that the Lumumba cabinet was the only legal Congolese government capable of ordering his ouster. Orders for immediate closure of the Ghanaian embassy had been issued by the Mobutu regime Nov. 18 but were amended by High Commission Pres. Bomboko, who cabled orders from UN headquarters Nov. 19 to limit the expulsions to Welbeck and a few aides. Welbeck was accused of having intervened in Congolese politics to bring about the restoration of Lumumba. Ghanaian Embassy Secy. Lovelace Mensah, who had been arrested Nov. 16 on charges of carrying funds and messages to Lumumba, was freed the next day and ordered ousted.

The firing reportedly began after Cols. Mobutu and N'Kokolo had gone to Welbeck's home with Congolese troops to order him to leave the country. The troops, estimated to number 300 Congolese and Tunisians, opened fire when Welbeck refused to leave his home. N'Kokolo reportedly was killed by the first shots. The firing continued until the next morning. Welbeck and Mensah were taken from the Ghanaian residence Nov. 22 by Lt. Gen. Henry T. Alexander, British commander of the Ghanaian army, and were driven to Ndjili Airport and put aboard a plane for Ghana. Alexander had flown to Leopoldville from Ghana Nov. 21 to tell Welbeck of his recall from the Congo post. 370 Ghanaian police serving with the UN Force were ordered withdrawn by Ghana Nov. 23. They left Leopoldville Nov. 27.

Congolese soldiers terrorized UN personnel in Leopoldville Nov. 22 in retaliation for the death of N'Kokolo. UN employes were dragged from their cars and homes and were detained and beaten before Congolese officers succeeded in restoring partial order.

LUMUMBA IMPRISONED

Mobutu Regime Acts Against Foe

Lumumba was arrested in Mweka, near Port Francqui, Kasai Province Dec. 1 after he had fled Leopoldville in an apparent effort to reach his supporters in Oriental Province.

Lumumba had evaded cordons of Congolese and Moroccan UN troops guarding his Leopoldville home and had slipped out of the city Nov. 28. The UN Force reported his departure Nov. 29 and withdrew the UN guards. The Mobutu government charged the UN with aiding Lumumba's escape and ordered a nationwide army and police search for Lumumba Nov. 29 to prevent him from reaching Stanleyville. The UN denied any complicity in the escape.

Lumumba was returned to Leopoldville by plane Dec. 2 and was imprisoned at Mobutu's headquarters in suburban Binza. He was jeered at and beaten by Congolese soldiers as he was driven in an open truck from Ndjili Airport to Binza. 3 members of Lumumba's most recent cabinet, Information Min. Anicet Kashamura, Labor Min. Joachim Masena, State Min. Georges Grenfell reportedly were arrested and returned to Leopoldville with him.

Mobutu told newsmen Dec. 2 that Lumumba would be tried on charges of abusing his powers and inciting an army rebellion.

Secy. Gen. Hammarskjold cabled Pres. Kasavubu Dec. 2 to appeal for treatment of Lumumba according to "due process of law." In a 2d message sent to Kasavubu Dec. 2 after conferring with leaders of the 46-nation Afro-Asian UN bloc, Hammarskjold expressed UN concern at Lumumba's arrest. Rajeshwar Dayal reported to Hammarskjold Dec. 5 that Lumumba had suffered "serious injuries" from a beating inflicted by Congolese soldiers after his capture. Dayal said that Lumumba's head had been shaven and that he was being kept manacled under inhumane conditions. Hammarskjold cabled Kasavubu again Dec. 5 to ask that International

Red Cross representatives be allowed to see Lumumba. He reminded Kasavubu that Lumumba had been charged with no crime and was entitled to Parliamentary immunity from arrest. He warned that "world public opinion" would watch Lumumba's treatment. The State Department announced Dec. 6 that U.S. appeals for "humane treatment" and a "fair trial" for Lumumba had been sent to Kasavubu and Mobutu.

Mobutu refused Dec. 6 to let UN or Red Cross representatives visit Lumumba. He conceded that Lumumba had been mistreated after his arrest, but he said the mistreatment had been halted on his orders.

Lumumba Forces Launch Drive

The capture and imprisonment of Lumumba resulted in renewed fighting between his supporters and troops of the Mobutu regime as "Lumumbist" groups seized control of Oriental Province in the first step of a campaign to win control of the entire Congo.

Control of Oriental Province was assumed Dec. 4 in Stanleyville by Bernard Salumu, a leftist and former secretary to Lumumba. Salumu declared himself "commissioner of the Eastern [Oriental] district." He named Jean-Foster Manzilala as president of an independent provincial government. Salumu announced that his government was "seceding from the Leopoldville regime." Oriental military forces closed the province's frontiers, and no whites were permitted to leave without Salumu's specific authorization. It was reported from Leopoldville Dec. 5 that Oriental forces had attacked villages in Equator Province.

At least 9 persons were reported killed in fighting between Lumumbist tribesmen and Congolese troops Dec. 3-4 in Kikwit, Leopoldville Province, after the troops began arresting persons believed to have sheltered Lumumba. Moroccan UN troops were ordered to halt the Kikwit fighting Dec. 4.

Lumumba's supporters in Oriental Province threatened Dec. 7 to round up all Belgians and other whites in Stanleyville and to "start cutting off the heads of some of them" unless Lumumba were freed within 48 hours. The ultima-

tum, cabled to Kasavubu by Salumu and disclosed in Leopoldville Dec. 9, said: "It is unacceptable that the Congo
is recolonized by Belgian imperialists. Will sabotage all
Belgian interests if Lumumba not released. . . ." The UN
command ordered Ethiopian UN troops in Stanleyville Dec.
9 to give "all effective protection" to Europeans in the
city. It was reported from Stanleyville Dec. 9-10 that hundreds of the 1,000 whites in the city were under UN Force
protection in a school compound. A UN mission headed by
Brig. Mangasha Iyassu of Ethiopia, UN Force chief of staff,
flew to Stanleyville Dec. 10 to supervise UN protective measures and to meet with Salumu and Manzilala. A similar
mission was carried out by the consuls of the U.S., France,
West Germany and other states. No action was taken against
the province's white residents despite the threats voiced by
the Lumumbist leader.

Gizenga Proclaims Rebel Regime

A new Congolese government was proclaimed in Stanleyville Dec. 13 by Antoine Gizenga, allegedly pro-Comm-
unist deputy premier in the former Lumumba cabinet. In a
message cabled to Soviet Rep.-to-UN Zorin, Security Council president for December, Gizenga said that the Congo's
"lawful government" had been moved from Leopoldville to
Stanleyville and that he had assumed the premiership left
vacant by Lumumba's arrest. Gizenga claimed the loyalty
of 3,000 troops in Stanleyville and of 3,000 elsewhere in
Oriental Province.

In Leopoldville, UN officials told newsmen Dec. 13 that
Gizenga's proclamation had increased the "potential civil
war situation" despite the Mobutu-Kasavubu regime's inability to launch an attack on Oriental Province. It was reported Dec. 14 that arms had been delivered to the Stanleyville regime from an unknown source aboard Soviet aircraft. Statements broadcast Dec. 15 by the Mobutu regime
charged that the USSR was the leader of an Asian-African
plot to take over "parts of the Congo" with the Stanleyville
regime. The UAR, Sudan, Ghana, Guinea, Morocco, Indonesia and Ceylon were accused of aiding the alleged conspiracy.

A total blockade of Oriental Province was ordered Dec. 20 by the Mobutu government.

UN Force Members Threaten to Quit

At least 6 of the 18 nations that had contributed troops for the UN Force ordered or threatened to order the withdrawal of their contingents from the Congo Dec. 7-12. The withdrawals were threatened in protest against the UN Force's alleged partisanship in the Congo crisis, particularly its supposed support of the Mobutu-Kasavubu regime against Lumumba.

Yugoslav Rep.-to-UN Dobrivoje Vidic informed Hammarskjold in New York Dec. 7 that Yugoslavia's troops were being recalled because the UN Force had aided the "armed suppression of the people's revolt against foreign intervention." UAR Pres. Gamal Abdel Nasser's office said in Cairo Dec. 7 that the UAR's 520-man contingent was being withdrawn in retaliation for the Kasavubu regime's severance of relations with his government. (Kasavubu, in a letter to Nasser, demanded Dec. 1 that the UAR recall its embassy staff from Leopoldville on the ground that it had plotted with Lumumba against his government. The departure of Ghanaian diplomats from the Congo, requested in November, was completed Dec. 3. Ghana broke relations with Belgium Dec. 5 because of Belgium's alleged responsibility for the rupture between Ghana and the Congo.)

The withdrawal of Ceylon's 11-man UN Force contingent was ordered Dec. 7 by Prime Min. Sirimavo Bandaranaika, but the order was delayed Dec. 10 after a plea from Ghana Pres. Nkrumah. Indonesian Foreign Min. Subandrio announced Dec. 10 that Indonesia's 1,150-man UN contingent would be withdrawn because the UN Force had "failed" in its Congo mission. The recall of Morocco's 3,257-man contingent, the UN Force's largest, was ordered Dec. 12 on grounds that the force had failed to prevent Lumumba's arrest and no longer was being used to uphold the Congo's "legal authorities." Guinean Pres. Toure cabled the UN Security Council Dec. 12 that Guinea's 400 men were being recalled because UN Force actions in the Congo were contrary to the UN Charter.

USSR Demands Lumumba Release

A series of statements issued by the Soviet Union beginning Dec. 2 denounced the Western powers and Secy. Gen. Hammarskjold as responsible for Lumumba's arrest. The statements demanded Lumumba's release.

A Soviet UN mission statement charged Dec. 2 that Lumumba's arrest was the consequence of actions undertaken by the "illegal dictatorial Mobutu regime," Belgium and its "NATO allies," and the UN command in the Congo. It demanded that Hammarskjold fulfill his responsibility for Lumumba's safety. A Soviet government statement broadcast Dec. 5 by Moscow radio demanded (1) the release of Lumumba and restoration of his government, (2) UN action to disarm Mobutu's troops, (3) investigation of military and financial support given Mobutu, (4) expulsion of all Belgians from the Congo, (5) renewed UN debate on the Congo crisis.

NEW UN ACTION BLOCKED

USSR Vetoes Hammarskjold Powers

The UN Security Council was called into session Dec. 7 by the USSR to debate the crisis caused by the imprisonment of Lumumba. The Council was prevented by the USSR's 92d veto Dec. 14 from granting increased powers to Hammarskjold to deal with the situation. The Council was summoned by Soviet Rep.-to-UN Zorin to debate his government's demands for the release of Lumumba and his restoration to power. Zorin, who rejected U.S. demands that he disqualify himself as December Council president because of his past attacks on UN Congo policy, presented a Soviet draft resolution Dec. 7 embodying provisions of the 5-point Soviet declaration broadcast Dec. 5. Zorin Dec. 8 attacked Hammarskjold for using the UN Force to assist "hired assassins, directed by Mobutu," responsible for Lumumba's downfall.

Amb. James J. Wadsworth charged Dec. 9 that the USSR's main purpose in seeking Lumumba's release was to aggravate "chaos in the Congo" and to increase the chances of "Soviet domination." Wadsworth said Lumumba's arrest was a matter of "internal Congolese jurisdiction" and within the rights of the Kasavubu government. Sir Claude Corea, Ceylonese UN delegate, called on the Council Dec. 10 to give Hammarskjold authority to restore order in the Congo. Corea said the UN Force had not been sent to the Congo "merely to stand by."

A Western resolution that would have reaffirmed UN support for Hammarskjold's actions in the Congo was vetoed by Zorin Dec. 14. The Western resolution was supported by 7 Council members and was opposed by the USSR, Poland and Ceylon (Tunisia abstained). The Soviet draft introduced Dec. 7 by Zorin was rejected by 8-2 Dec. 14 (USSR and Poland in favor, Ceylon abstaining). A compromise Tunisian-Ceylonese draft was withdrawn Dec. 14 when it became clear that it lacked enough votes for adoption.

Hammarskjold, in an impassioned defense of his Congo actions, warned the Council Dec. 14 that if the UN were forced to end its military and aid operations in the Congo "the consequences would be immediate civil war, degenerating into tribal conflicts fought in the most uninhibited manner." He asserted that other nations then could be expected to intervene, creating a "Spanish war situation." He warned that in Kasai Province alone, there were "200 people dying daily from sheer starvation." A UN withdrawal, he said, would bring the "total collapse" of the Congolese nation.

Assembly Debates Problem

General Assembly debate on the Congo was renewed Dec. 16 at the request of India and Yugoslavia after the Security Council's failure to reach agreement on the problem.

A draft resolution presented to the Assembly Dec. 16 by Yugoslavia and 6 Afro-Asian nations proposed UN action to (a) liberate all Congolese political prisoners, including Lumumba, (b) reconvene the Congolese Parliament as the country's sole legal political institution, (c) "prevent . . . any interference in the political life of the country" by the armed forces of the Mobutu regime or any other groups. The proposal was considered an attempt to restore Lumumba to power through the Congolese Parliament while Mobutu's troops were prevented from acting by the UN Force. A 2d proposal, submitted Dec. 16 by Francisco Milla Bermudez of Honduras, urged the Assembly to grant Hammarskjold special powers for a period of 100 days to launch a final UN effort to restore peace in the Congo.

A U.S.-British draft resolution was presented to the Assembly Dec. 19. It called on Hammarskjold "to continue to discharge the mandate entrusted to him by the United Nations" and (a) urged him to continue his "vigorous efforts" to bar foreign military personnel from the Congo, (b) asked all UN states to refrain from military aid to the Congo except through the UN command, (c) directed reconvening of the Congolese Parliament, (d) urged support for Pres. Kasavubu's intended round-table conference of Congo political leaders and (e) proposed measures to assure the safety of Lumumba.

Hammarskjold warned the Assembly Dec. 19 that unless it produced a clear decision on future UN Congo policy, "I would have to put up to the Security Council the question of whether the United Nations Force should withdraw." Hammarskjold held that Assembly failure to strengthen his Congo mandate would condemn him to remain a "passive witness" while the Congo slipped into civil war as a result of the UN's inaction. He could not, he said, continue UN Congo operations under these conditions.

The 2 major draft resolutions were voted on by the Assembly Dec. 20, but each failed to win the required 2/3 majority. The Western resolution received 43 votes, one short of the required number, but was opposed by 22 nations (32 abstainers were recorded, including France and most African French Community states). The Yugoslav-Asian-African resolution was supported by 28 nations and opposed by 42; 27 nations abstained.

Hammarskjold told the Assembly following the voting that it and the Security Council, by their "dual failure" to adopt a new Congo policy, had confirmed the existence of a serious "split in the organization on this issue."

He said, "The previous resolutions on the Congo remain fully valid, and so do . . . all the obligations they impose on all member nations." "Naturally," he declared, the UN Congo operation "will be continued under the previous decisions."

The Assembly adopted without opposition Dec. 20 a motion to keep the Congo question on its agenda when it met again in 1961 to complete its regular 15th annual session.

Congo's Leaders Confer

Chiefs of the Congolese and Katanga governments and of rival political factions met Dec. 18-20 in Brazzaville, capital of the (former French) Congo Republic across the Congo River from Leopoldville. Participants in the meeting, held during a Brazzaville conference of African French Community states, included Pres. Kasavubu, High Commission Pres. Bomboko, Katanga Pres. Tshombe and Albert Kalonji of South Kasai. No agreements were announced after the meeting, but Tshombe told newsmen Dec. 20 that participants had accepted an invitation to talks in Elisabethville in 1961.

(Tshombe had flown to Brussels Dec. 5 to confer with Belgian leaders but had failed to win Belgian recognition for an independent Katanga government. Belgian Foreign Min. Wigny Dec. 7 rejected allegations that the official reception accorded Tshombe constituted recognition. Tshombe, however, announced on his return to Elisabethville Dec. 10 that Katanga's independence had become a "reality.")

McKeown Heads UN Force

Maj. Gen. Sean McKeown, chief of staff of the Irish Army, was named Dec. 21 by Secy. Gen. Hammarskjold to replace Maj. Gen. Carl Carlsson von Horn of Sweden as commander of the UN Force in the Congo. Von Horn was said to have resigned for health reasons.

Sture C. Linner, head of UN civil operations in the Congo, warned Dec. 22 that at least 300,000 refugees from tribal warfare were dependent on UN food in South Kasai

and that "thousands" were in imminent danger of starvation. Linner reported that hundreds of Africans were dying from hunger each day in the Bakwanga area of South
Kasai and that an emergency UN food airlift would be begun to the region. UPI reported Dec. 22 that the starving
Africans were largely Balubas driven into remote areas
of Kasai by their tribal enemies, the Luluas.

(It was reported Dec. 28 that 20 persons were killed
and many others raped and injured when Baluba tribesmen
attacked a UN Force-protected train carrying 100 school
children and 200 other persons from Elisabethville to
western Katanga. The report was denied, however, by Irish
UN troops, who said that the attacking Balubas had retreated at the sight of UN troops. At least 100 Baluba tribesmen were reported to have been killed in attacks on UN
units and Katanga police in northern Katanga Dec. 4-10.
30 Balubas had been killed in attacks on Nigerian UN troops
in northern Katanga Nov. 29, and the bodies of 80 slain in
tribal warfare had been discovered by UN troops near
Langwe, Katanga Nov. 18.)

Lumumbists Raid Kivu

Pro-Lumumba troops from Oriental Province captured and abducted Kivu Provincial Premier Jean Miruho,
3 members of his cabinet and Maj. Singa, commander of
the Kivu garrison, in a raid Dec. 25 on Bukavu, capital
of Kivu. The assault was carried out by 60 Congolese soldiers in jeeps and military vehicles. (One Nigerian UN soldier and 10 Congolese had been killed in Bukavu Dec. 16
when UN troops were forced to attack the Congolese to
free a 52-member Austrian medical team detained as Belgian spies.)

It was reported in Stanleyville Dec. 26 that Egyptian
army officers had been identified in the military entour-
age of Premier Gizenga, head of the regime in Stanleyville. The UN Force blocked Stanleyville airport to incom-
ing flights Dec. 31 after it was reported that Soviet Ilyu-
shin transports had been observed landing supplies in other
parts of Oriental Province and would begin aid deliveries
directly to the Lumumbist regime in Stanleyville.

Col. Mobutu told newsmen in Luluabourg Dec. 30 that he would restore government control over Bukavu and other areas of Kivu Province said to be in the hands of Lumumbist forces. 5 planeloads of government paratroops left Luluabourg for Usumbura, Ruanda-Urundi Dec. 31, en route to Kivu to launch an offensive against the rebels.

1961

Full-scale civil war gripped the Congo in 1961 after the murder of Premier Lumumba, apparently at the hands of the secessionist Katanga Province regime. Its mandate strengthened, the UN Force backed the central government in its efforts to put down the dissident movements led by Antoine Gizenga, former aide to Lumumba, and Moise Tshombe, the Katangan president. A new Leopoldville government, headed by Cyrille Adoula, took office and sought to negotiate a political settlement with the dissident movements. When these efforts failed, the UN Force again attacked in Katanga, seriously weakening but not destroying the secessionist regime. The UN action gave rise to bitter international debate over the morality of the use of arms by the world peace organization. Among the casualties of the Congolese rebellion in 1961: UN Secy. Gen. Dag Hammarskjold, killed in the crash of his plane as he flew to peace talks with Katangan leaders.

POLITICAL STRIFE CONTINUES

Ruanda Border Clashes

Armed clashes took place Jan. 1 and 13, 1961 between opposing Congolese military forces on the border between the Belgian-administered Ruanda-Urundi UN trust territory and Kivu Province, in the Congo Republic. The fighting involved troops of the central Congolese government of Col. Joseph D. Mobutu and Pres. Joseph Kasavubu and rebel forces backing imprisoned former Premier Patrice Lumumba.

The Mobutu troops reportedly had been airlifted Dec. 31, 1960 from Luluabourg, Kasai Province, to Usumbura, capital of Ruanda-Urundi, to attack Lumumbist forces dominating Kivu Province. The central government force, numbering 100 men and 3 officers, was driven to Shangugu, on the Kivu border and was fired on by pro-Lumumba troops when it sought to cross into Kivu. It was reported Jan. 1 that the Mobutu troops had retreated into Ruanda-Urundi after 23 had been wounded and 60 had been taken prisoner. A 2d Ruanda-Urundi clash occurred Jan. 13 when rebel Congolese crossed the border from the Goma district of Kivu Province and fought with Belgian troops based in Kisenyi. The Congolese withdrew to Kivu Jan. 14, reportedly taking 12 Belgian prisoners. UN spokesmen reported Jan. 15 that 3 of the Belgians had died of wounds.

UN Secy. Gen. Dag Hammarskjold protested to Belgium Jan. 1 over the Mobutu troops' use of Ruanda-Urundi for "transit purposes in support of military action." The UN Security Council met Jan. 12 to hear Soviet Deputy Foreign Min. Valerian A. Zorin charge Belgium with aggression for its alleged support of the Kivu raid through Ruanda. The USSR demanded that Belgium be condemned and deprived of the Ruanda trusteeship. The Council adjourned Jan. 14 after voting by 4 to 0 (USSR, Ceylon, Liberia and UAR in favor; all 7 other states abstaining), 3 short of a necessary majority, on a resolution requesting consideration of the Soviet demand by a session of the General Assembly.

Hammarskjold Mission to Congo

Secy. Gen. Hammarskjold left New York for the Congo Jan. 3 to confer with Congolese leaders and with members of his 11-nation UN Conciliation Commission on the Congo. (The Conciliation Commission, headed by Jaja Wachuku of Nigeria, had begun assembling in the Congo Jan. 2. The commission was composed of non-European nations that had contributed UN Force troops, with the exception of Guinea, Mali, Indonesia and the UAR, which had resigned after the UN General Assembly's recognition of the Kasavubu government in 1960.) Hammarskjold was met on his arrival in Leopoldville Jan. 4 by Congolese demonstrators shouting demands for the release of ex-Premier Lumumba and for the reconvening of the Lumumba-dominated Congolese Parliament. He was guarded by Malayan UN Force troops as he met with the Conciliation Commission and then conferred with Rajeshwar Dayal of India, his personal representative in the Congo. Hammarskjold met with Pres. Kasavubu Jan. 5 and left the Congo Jan. 6 for South Africa.

Rebels Invade Katanga

The UN command reported Jan. 9 that Congolese forces commanded by Lumumbist officers had invaded northern Katanga and had been welcomed by Baluba tribesmen engaged in a rebellion against Pres. Moise Tshombe's regime. The rebels, totaling 1,500, were followers of Antoine Gizenga's dissident Stanleyville regime. The invaders were accompanied by a civilian group planning to form a Luluaba Province government under Remy Mwamba, former justice minister in the Lumumba cabinet. Luluaba Province, as proclaimed by the pro-Lumumba group, covered 2/3 of Katanga. Mwamba and Prosper Ilunga, a Baluba political leader, established their capital in Manono, Katanga.

The Katanga government announced Jan. 12 that Pres. Tshombe had renounced a UN-imposed truce covering northern Katanga and that the Katanga air force had attacked the invaders. Heavy fighting was reported in the vicinity of Albertville. Despite the Katanga countermeasure, Gizenga's troops were reported to have seized much of northern Katanga by Jan. 29. UN troops were withdrawn from Luena, 250 miles northwest of Elisabethville, after failing to stop the fighting. The fall of Manono was confirmed Jan. 30 with the news that Katanga planes had bombed the city.

Lumumba Shifted to Katanga

The transfer of ex-Premier Lumumba from a military prison in Thysville, near Leopoldville, to a prison in Jadotville, in Katanga Province, was announced Jan. 18 by the central Congolese and Katanga governments. The transfer was said to have been ordered because the Thysville prison did not provide "sufficient guarantees."

Lumumba and 2 of his supporters imprisoned with him, ex-Youth Min. Maurice Mpolo and Senate Vice Pres. Joseph Okito, were flown to Elisabethville and driven to Jadotville Jan. 17. UN troops who witnessed the transfer reported that Lumumba and the 2 others were beaten repeatedly and that UN troops had been ordered not to intervene. Secy. Gen. Hammarskjold said Jan. 24 that he had urged Pres. Kasavubu to return Lumumba to Leopoldville to participate in planned political talks; Hammarskjold advised that Kasavubu "have Lumumba returned from Katanga and . . . unless released, he be given the opportunity to answer the charges against him in a fair and public hearing by an impartial tribunal."

UN headquarters in Leopoldville Jan. 20 confirmed reports that pro-Lumumba forces controlling Oriental and Kivu Province had arrested and beaten Europeans and attacked some Congolese for Lumumba's transfer to Katanga. 12 Belgians were arrested in Stanleyville Jan. 20 and were released the next day only after payment of a $10,000 ransom to officials of the Gizenga regime. Warnings were transmitted to Lumumbist groups in Oriental and Kivu Provinces Jan. 21 by Rajeshwar Dayal that the UN Force would not tolerate arbitrary arrests of Europeans. The UN Command announced Jan. 26 that it would help transport all whites wanting to leave endangered districts.

UN Force Weakened

A warning that the recall of UN Force troop contingents might make it necessary to end the UN's Congo operations was laid before the Security Council Jan. 26 by Secy. Gen. Hammarskjold. Hammarskjold reported that Yugoslavia and Guinea had ordered their contingents withdrawn and that 3 more nations—the UAR, Indonesia and Morocco—had informed him of their "definite decisions" to recall their troops. The formal request for withdrawal of the 497-man UAR contingent was received by the UN Jan. 23. The UAR troops were airlifted from the Congo Jan. 31. It was announced simultaneously that Morocco's 3,132-man unit had been removed from UN control and was to assemble for transport home. 1,149 Indonesian and 738 Guinean soldiers were awaiting transportation and Ireland's contingent had been reduced from 1,397 men to one battalion of 655 soldiers.

The Security Council resumed its debate on the Congo Feb. 1 to hear Congo Pres. Kasavubu's demand that Hammarskjold be directed to use UN troops against Lumumbist rebels. The session also heard neutralist appeals for the release of Lumumba and a renewed request by Secy. Gen. Hammarskjold for increased power to deal with the Congo situation. The Council took no immediate action on any of these questions. Hammarskjold, addressing the Council Feb. 1, asked for greater powers to prevent "the threatening possibility of civil war." He indicated that if he was given a stronger mandate, he would attempt to disarm the troops commanded by the central Congolese government and by rival Lumumbist groups in order to remove the Congolese army from politics. Hammarskjold insisted that the UN Force could not be used to support Kasavubu's regime against the rebels without scrapping the limited mandate under which it had been sent to the Congo.

(Col. Mobutu warned in Leopoldville Feb. 3 that the UN would be "playing with fire" if it attempted to disarm Congolese government forces. Pres. Tshombe declared Feb. 7 that any such action against Katangan forces would be reagarded as a declaration of war.)

Ileo Forms New Congo Regime

A new provisional Congolese government headed by Senate Pres. Joseph Ileo was installed in Leopoldville Feb. 9 by Pres. Kasavubu. The new government replaced the military regime and College of High Commissioners proclaimed in 1960 by Mobutu. (Kasavubu had promoted Mobutu to major general Jan. 23 and had named him commander-in-chief of Congolese forces.)

In his decree establishing the new government, Kasavubu said the Congolese Parliament would be reconvened "as soon as possible." He said he had acted under the Congo's provisional constitution in naming the new cabinet before reconvening Parliament. He asserted that Congolese armed forces had restored enough order so that the interim Mobutu regime no longer was needed. Ileo had been named premier by Kasavubu in 1960 but had been prevented from taking office by the political struggle among Kasavubu, Lumumba, and Mobutu. His new cabinet was composed mainly of pro-Kasavubu politicians, but some posts were left vacant for later appointments from Katanga and provinces held by Lumumbist forces.

The new cabinet: Premier—Ileo; Vice Premier and Information Min.—Jean Bolikango; Interior— Cyrille Adoula; Foreign Affairs and Foreign Trade—Justin Bomboko; Finance—Pascal Nkayi; Education—Cleophas Bizala; Labor—Felicien Kimvay; Economic Affairs—Jean-Pierre Dericoyard; Planning and Coordination—Alois Kabangi; Public Works—Alphonse Ilunga; Agriculture—Francois Mopipi; Civil Service—Paul Bolya; Resident Min. in Belgium—Albert Delvaux; Social Affairs—Jacques Massa; State Min. for Semi-Government Workers—Charles Kisolokela.

LUMUMBA MURDERED

Katanga Responsibility Charged

The murder of ex-Premier Lumumba by Congolese tribesmen was announced Feb. 12 by the government of Katanga Province, where Lumumba had been transferred as a prisoner. According to Katanga's story of the murder,

Lumumba, Maurice Mpolo and Joseph Okito escaped and were slain as they fled toward an area of Katanga held by troops of the Lumumbist Gizenga regime. This account was, however, contradicted by a report issued later in 1961 by a UN committee formed to investigate the murders. The UN group said Lumumba had been shot immediately after his transfer to Katanga by direct order of Pres. Tshombe.

The alleged escape of Lumumba and of the 2 former government officials held with him at an isolated farm near Mutshatsha, 200 miles west of Elisabethville, was reported Feb. 10 by Katanga radio and by Katanga Interior Min. Godefroid Munongo in a message to the UN Command. Lumumba, Mpolo and Okito were said to have overpowered Katanga sentries guarding them Feb. 9 and to have fled in a police car. Katanga's armed forces were reported to have begun a ground-air search for the fugitives Feb. 10. The car was said to have been abandoned and wrecked Feb. 11 near Kasaji. The announcement of Lumumba's escape aroused fears that he had been slain by the Katanga government and that the story of the prison break had been fabricated to conceal his death. A UN investigation of the circumstances of Lumumba's escape was ordered by Secy. Gen. Hammarskjold Feb. 10 but was rejected by the Katanga government Feb. 12 on the ground that it was "an internal Katanga matter."

The Katanga government announced Feb. 13 that Lumumba and his 2 companions had been "massacred" by Katanga tribesmen Feb. 12 at an unnamed place some distance from where their escape car had been found. A communique issued by Munongo and broadcast by the Katanga radio said the bodies had been identified and buried on the spot. It said: The tribesmen and village would not be identified to bar reprisals or judicial action against them and to keep the grave from becoming a shrine; the villagers would be paid a 400,000-franc ($8,000) reward offered for Lumumba's capture after the announcement of his escape. Munongo said the UN had no "right to take positions in this matter." He said Lumumba was a "criminal on political, not judicial grounds," who was responsible for the deaths of thousands of Katangans. He declared: "If people accuse us of killing Lumumba, I will reply: 'Prove it.' "

Anti-Belgian Reaction to Slaying

The news of Lumumba's slaying brought an immediate reaction from Communist, Asian and African countries, where the murder was blamed on the UN and the Western powers, particularly Belgium. Condemnations of the Lumumba slaying were issued by many governments, particularly Communist China, Cuba, Morocco, and others that had supported Lumumba. A statement issued Feb. 13 by Pres. John F. Kennedy expressed "great shock" at the slaying.

Demonstrators attacked and smashed windows of the Belgian embassies in Cairo Feb. 12, Rome Feb. 13, and Moscow Feb. 14. The Moscow demonstration was staged by 6,000 persons, many of them Africans studying at the USSR's new Friendship University. A mob of 30,000 attacked and ransacked the embassy in Belgrade the same day. Other anti-Belgian demonstrations were reported Feb. 14 from Warsaw, London, New Delhi and many Asian and African capitals; large crowds also picketed the U.S. and French embassies. The demonstrations were resumed Feb. 15, when rioters attacked, ransacked and burned files of the Belgian embassies in Warsaw and Cairo. The Belgian embassy in Washington was pelted with eggs by Africans and American Negro students. Similar attacks were staged the same day on U.S. embassies in Cairo, Accra and other capitals. Belgium severed diplomatic relations with the UAR Feb. 25 in retaliation for the attacks on its Cairo embassy. Pres. Gamal Abdel Nasser responded Feb. 26 by ordering the sequestration of all Belgian property in the UAR and the expulsion of all Belgian residents.

UN Probe Demanded

Secy. Gen. Hammarskjold told the UN Security Council Feb. 13 that the deaths of Lumumba and his associates should be given a full and impartial "international investigation." U.S. Amb.-to-UN Adlai E. Stevenson backed

Hammarskjold's demand for a UN inquiry. He said the "distressing and deplorable . . . death of Mr. Lumumba without trial or judgment" was "sad testimony to the distance we will have to travel before our task there [in the Congo] will be completed." Soviet Rep.-to-UN Valerian A. Zorin denounced the slayings as a "grievous" crime of colonialism "committed under the blue flag of the United Nations." He rejected a UN inquiry because "we have not the slightest confidence in . . . [Hammarskjold] or in his staff."

But Katanga Pres. Tshombe announced Feb. 14 that he would not permit the UN to investigate the circumstances of Lumumba's death. He charged that Katanga had been at peace when he permitted the entry of UN troops, but that it since had been "bathed in fire and blood."

East Recognizes Gizenga

The first formal moves to recognize the Lumumbist government in Oriental Province were taken by the USSR and UAR Feb. 14. The USSR's action was disclosed in a Soviet government declaration and was confirmed in a message to Antoine Gizenga, described as "acting prime minister" of the Oriental government. The Soviet statements pledged unlimited aid to the Gizenga regime in its battle against the Kasavubu government. A similar statement by the UAR announced its recognition of Gizenga's regime as the "legitimate national government of the Congo." The Gizenga government was recognized by East Germany, Ghana and Yugoslavia Feb. 15.

In a prepared statement read to a Washington news conference Feb. 15, Pres. Kennedy warned that the U.S. would defend the UN Charter "by opposing any attempt by any government to intervene unilaterally in the Congo." Without directly mentioning the USSR, Mr. Kennedy said he was "seriously concerned at what appears to be a threat of unilateral intervention" in the Congo. He emphasized that "the United States had supported and will continue to support the United Nations presence in the Congo." The President denounced "the purported recognition of Congolese factions as so-called governments." He reiterated

U.S. support for the central Congolese governments as "the only legal authority" in the Congo.

Hostages Reported Slain

Retaliatory executions of political hostages held by the central Congolese government and the Gizenga regime were reported from the Congo Feb. 19-23. Maj. Gen. Victor Lundula had been credited with restraining his Lumumbist forces from retaliations against whites and Congolese immediately after Lumumba's death, but his efforts foundered after Lumumbist supporters themselves were shot by rival groups and followers of the central government.

The executions of 7 prominent Lumumbist prisoners were reported to the UN Command in Leopoldville Feb. 19 by Andre Kabaye, interior minister in the South Kasai regime led by Albert Kalonji. The 6 men, whose deaths were confirmed by Hammarskjold in a statement to the UN Security Council Feb. 20, were ex-Pres. Jean-Pierre Finant of Oriental Province, Maj. Jacques Fataki, former chief of Stanleyville military police, Gilbert Nzuzi, leader of the MNC youth movement, Pierre Elengesa, a leader of the Leopoldville Liberal Circle, and 2 officials identified only as Yangara and Muzunga. The execution of Jacques Lumbala, a member of the former Lumumba cabinet, was reported by the UN Command Feb. 21.

In a UN report Feb. 23 on conditions in Oriental and Kivu Provinces, Rajeshwar Dayal said that 14 political prisoners held by the Gizenga regime in Stanleyville had been killed in retaliation for the slayings of Lumumbists.

UN Report on Lumumba Murder

The Katanga version of Lumumba's death was rejected by a UN investigating commission in a report published Nov. 14. The commission declared that Lumumba probably had been murdered on the orders of the Katanga government, possibly in the presence of Pres. Tshombe, Interior Min. Godefroid Munongo and Foreign Min. Evariste Kimbe. It cited evidence that the execution had been carried out near Elisabethville Jan. 17, immediately after Lumumba's arrival in Katanga. The commission's members (Justice U Aung Khine of Burma, Salvador Martinez de Alva of Mexico, Ato Tashoma Hailemariam of Ethiopia, Avite d'Almeida of Togo) based their findings on UN documents and interrogations of unnamed witnesses—none of them present at the slaying—in London, Brussels and Geneva. The group had been prevented by the Congolese government from entering the Congo. The commission's findings:

(1) "The weight of evidence is against the official version of . . . Katanga Province that Mr. Lumumba, Mr. Okito and Mr. Mpolo were killed by certain tribesmen on 12 Feb. 1961." (2) "On the contrary, the commission accepts as substantially true . . . evidence indicating that the prisoners were killed on 17 Jan. 1961 after their arrival in a villa not far from Elisabethville and in all probability in the presence of high officials of . . . Katanga Province, namely Mr. Tshombe, Mr. Munongo and Mr. Kimbe, and that the escape story was staged." (3) "A great deal of suspicion is cast on a certain Col. [Carlos] Huyghe, a Belgian mercenary, as being the actual perpetrator of Mr. Lumumba's murder, which was committed in accordance with a prearranged plan. . . . " (4) "In view of the lack of confirmation," the commission considers that other evidence cited "should be treated with caution. ... " (5) " . . . Pres. Kasavubu and his aides . . . should not escape responsibility for the death of Mr. Lumumba . . . For Mr. Kasavubu and his aides had handed over Mr. Lumumba and his colleagues to the Katangan authorities knowing full well . . . that they were throwing them into the hands of their bitterest political enemies." "The [Katanga] government . . . contributed, directly or indirectly, to the murder." (6) "The record . . . bristles with evidence indicative of the extensive role played by Mr. Munongo . . . in the entire plot leading to the murder of Mr. Lumumba. . . . " "The commission again repeats that the attitude of the . . . Republic of the Congo had prevented it from going to the scene of the crime to carry out its investigation. ... "

Pres. Tshombe declared Nov. 16 that the UN commission's report and its accusations of his complicity in Lumumba's murder were "completely false."

UN AUTHORIZES MILITARY ACTION

Council Acts to Prevent Civil War

A resolution authorizing UN troops to use arms to prevent a full-scale civil war in the Congo was adopted Feb. 21 by the UN Security Council. The resolution, introduced Feb. 17 by Ceylon, Liberia and the UAR, was approved by a vote of 9-0 (USSR and France abstaining). It ordered UN troops to use force as a last resort to halt civil war. It also called for (a) insulation of the Congolese Army from politics, (b) the removal from the Congo of all Belgian and other foreign military and political personnel not employed by the UN, (c) settlement of Congolese political strife by the reconvening of Parliament and reconciliation of opposing political factions, (d) the fixing of responsibility for the murder of Lumumba.

The Council Feb. 21 rejected 2 other Congo resolutions. It voted by 8-1 (Ceylon and UAR abstaining) to defeat a Soviet draft demanding the disbanding of all UN operations in the Congo and the dismissal of Secy. Gen. Hammarskjold. It failed by one vote (6-0, with the U.S., Britain, France, China and Turkey abstaining) to give the 7 votes required for approval of an "emergency" Ceylon-Liberia-UAR resolution that would have authorized UN troops to use force to prevent the arrest, deportation or killing of Congolese political leaders.

Addressing the Council Feb. 21, after passage of the resolution authorizing UN military action, Hammarskjold appealed for further contributions of troops to strengthen the UN Force and enable it to fulfill its new mandate. Hammarskjold said the Council's action had given "a stronger and more clear framework for United Nations action" in the Congo. He again rebutted Soviet charges of his alleged responsibility for Lumumba's death, asserting that even direct UN intervention against the Katanga regime could not have saved Lumumba.

(The N.Y. Times reported Feb. 21 that UN Force strength had totaled 18,888 men Jan. 20, but that withdrawals of UAR, Moroccan and Guinean troop units had reduced that number to 16,653, and further withdrawals ordered by Indonesia and Morocco would reduce the original force to 13,363. A Malayan offer of 800 more troops, disclosed Feb. 18 by Hammarskjold's office, would raise the force to 14,163. Indian Prime Min. Jawaharlal Nehru had offered an unspecified number of troops Feb. 15. The promised Indian force, of 4,700 men, began arriving in the Congo Mar. 15 aboard U.S. military transports.)

USSR Asks Intervention by Africans

Soviet Premier Nikita S. Khrushchev, in messages Feb. 22 to Indian Prime Min. Nehru and the heads of 66 other governments, called for the formation of an all-African commission to replace the UN in the Congo and ᴊstore full "independence" to the country. Khrushchev's note to Nehru, made public Feb. 25, reiterated Soviet demands for the dismissal of Hammarskjold and his replacement by a 3-member UN executive board. Hammarskjold, Khrushchev charged, had dishonored his UN post by his role as "chief assassin" of Lumumba. The proposed Congo commission was to be made up of representatives of the African nations whose troops were serving with the UN Force in the Congo. The Khrushchev note demanded full support for the Gizenga government in Stanleyville. It called for the removal of Gen. Mobutu and Katanga Pres. Tshombe and their trial for complicity in Lumumba's murder.

Nehru said in New Delhi Feb. 27 that he opposed any attempt to reorganize the UN secretary general's office "at the present moment." He made clear his support for the Security Council's authorization for UN troops to use force in the Congo.

Pres. Kwame Nkrumah of Ghana had proposed Feb. 18 that a new all–African UN Force be sent to the Congo and be given full responsibility for the restoration of law and order. Nkrumah, in a message cabled to Hammarskjold, warned that the continued flow of arms and munitions into the Congo could "lead to a civil war of the Spanish type, with grave consequences." Nkrumah said that "in my view the interpretation of the Security Council mandate, namely noninterference in the internal affairs of the Congo, is no longer tenable." He declared that "from now on the initiative must come from the African countries with military support from the Asian bloc."

Provisions of Nkrumah's proposal: (1) establishment of a new "African" UN command with "complete responsibility for law and order in the Congo"; (2) the disarming and reorganizing of all Congolese armed forces, by force if necessary; (3) expulsion of all non-Africans serving with Congolese armed forces; (4) the release of all political prisoners and convening of the Congolese Parliament by the new UN command; (5) the temporary departure from the Congo of all "foreign diplomatic missions and representatives."

Congo Leaders Balk, Warned by UN

Premier Ileo warned Feb. 22 that his newly-installed central Congolese government would oppose, by force if necessary, implementation of the Security Council's Congo resolution. Ileo, holding his first news conference since becoming premier, asserted that "if they [UN Force commanders] mean to disarm our army, that will be a declaration of war." "We are ready to defend ourselves." A general mobilization was ordered in Katanga Province Feb. 21 by Pres. Tshombe to prevent the UN Force from carrying out the resolution. Tshombe charged the Council action was "a veritable declaration of war on Katanga and on the whole of the former Belgian Congo."

The Congolese leaders were warned by Hammarskjold Feb. 27 that he intended to back with force the Council's orders to halt the unrest in the Congo. Hammarskjold's message, reportedly duplicated in letters to Tshombe and Gizenga, was addressed to Pres. Kasavubu. It said: "The world is no longer willing nor in a position to accept the consequences of the continued splits, abetted by outside interests, which divide the country. Reconciliation on a nationwide scale is . . . imperative, and anyone . . . refusing to make his full and selfless contribution to such a reconciliation shoulders a heavy responsibility." The UN would be backed by all "the strength needed," Hammarskjold's message declared.

(Congolese soldiers made a series of attacks on UN troops and personnel in the Leopoldville area Feb. 26-27. They arrested and then released some Tunisian and Danish soldiers, raped a UN civilian worker and beat 4 Canadian soldiers. The UN command, denouncing the attacks Feb. 27, warned that UN troops would use "full force" to prevent further incidents.)

Gizenga Forces Start Offensive

300 Congolese troops supporting the Stanleyville regime seized control of Luluabourg, capital of Kasai Province, Feb. 24 in what initially appeared to be a major offensive against the Kasavubu government. The Gizenga troops inexplicably were withdrawn from Luluabourg within a few days. Troops of the central government retook the city Feb. 28 and were reported to have killed 44 Congolese civilians in retaliation for pro-Lumumba rioting.

The Lumumbist forces had marched north into Kasai after an unsuccessful attempt to invade Katanga. UN spokemen said they had taken control of the Kasai capital without incident after the 1,000-man Luluabourg garrison, formerly believed loyal to Pres. Kasavubu, had agreed to "merge" with the invaders. Col. Mjoko, Luluabourg commander for the central government, was granted protection by Ghanaian UN troops stationed in the city. It was reported Feb. 25 that a 2d column of Lumumbist troops had marched from Stanleyville to Ikela and then northwest to Boende in an apparent drive on Coquilhatville, Equator Province. A 3d column of 500 rebel soldiers was reported Feb. 26 to have reached Port Francqui, on the Kasai River, 350 miles east of Leopoldville on the border of Leopoldville Province.

Despite the unexplained withdrawal from Luluabourg, the advances made by the rebels were believed to have assured their control of 3 provinces.

The UN Command Feb. 25 rejected a Kasavubu ultimatum that it act against the advancing Gizenga troops. The UN held that the rebels had advanced without fighting, persuading government troops to join them, and that there were no grounds for UN intervention against them.

Anti-Lumumbist Coalition Formed

The 3 major anti-Lumumbist groups—the central Congolese government and the secessionist regimes of South Kasai and Katanga Provinces—signed an agreement Feb. 28 in Elisabethville establishing "a common bloc against the danger of UN trusteeship, Communist tyranny and a Korean-style war" in the Congo.

The pact, signed by Presidents Kalonji of South Kasai and Tshombe of Katanga and Premier Ileo of the Leopoldville government, provided for a "common organization" to "pool" their military efforts to end the Congo crisis. A communique said that the agreements were "not directed as such against the government of Oriental and Kivu Provinces, but they do denounce the danger of Communist tyranny over the whole of the Congo." The pact was the first effort to unify the anti-Lumumbist groups, said to control 13,000 troops. The 3 leaders announced Feb. 28 that they had invited Gizenga, Gen. Lundula and their aides to a planned meeting of all Congolese factions in Tananarive, Madagascar.

(Katanga's agreement with the UN to freeze all troop movements was renounced Feb. 27 by Tshombe in reaction to the UN's failure to halt the advance of Lumumbists on Katanga. A UN note transmitted to Katanga Mar. 3 by Rajeshwar Dayal warned that UN troops would remain in Katanga until all Belgians were withdrawn in conformity with UN Security Council resolutions. The UN message demanded that Katanga take immediate steps to dismiss Belgians serving in its government and armed forces. Belgian officials reported in Brussels Mar. 11 that steps had been taken to implement the Security Council's demand for the withdrawal of Belgian personnel from the Congo. They said that Belgian military personnel had been ordered to return from the Congo, that all Belgian recruiting centers for Congo service had been closed, and that Belgian civilian officials had been given guarantees of jobs at home if they left the Congo. Of the 40,000 Belgians currently in the Congo, 2,000 were said to be working as civil officials for various Congolese governments, and 330 were said to be holding military posts.)

Government Troops Attack UN Posts

Fighting broke out Mar. 3-4 between Congolese troops commanded by the Kasavubu government and Sudanese UN Force contingents in Banana, on the Congo's narrow Atlantic coast, and in Matadi, Congo River port. The UN surrendered both cities and was virtually without port facilities in the Congo until Apr. 27, when it reached agreement with the Kasavubu government on reoccupation of UN posts in the cities.

The fighting began in Banana Mar. 3 when the Sudanese captured 2 Congolese attempting to arrest a UN radio operator. The Sudanese were fired on as they sought to return the Congolese prisoners. Acting under their new orders to use force if necessary, the Sudanese shot back and killed one of the Congolese. Heavy fighting broke out in the city and the Sudanese were withdrawn Mar. 4. The Matadi fighting broke out Mar. 4 and ended with the UN garrison's surrender and expulsion Mar. 5. (The U.S. confirmed Mar. 6 that a naval task force carrying 500 marines had been diverted to Congo waters to aid the UN withdrawal from Matadi but had resumed its voyage to South Africa after it no longer was needed.)

Secy. Gen. Hammarskjold protested the Banana fighting and recent attacks on UN personnel in Leopoldville in a cable to Pres. Kasavubu Mar. 4. Hammarskjold warned again that the UN would be forced to use arms if Congolese troops were used to frustrate UN efforts to restore order in the Congo. Rajeshwar Dayal met with Congolese Foreign Min. Bomboko Mar. 6 to demand that Matadi and Banana be returned to UN Force control. UN-Congo exchanges on the Banana-Matadi incident continued for nearly 2 months, until the Apr. 27 agreement.

CONGO CONFEDERATION PLANNED

Leaders Meet in Madagascar

Plans for a new confederation of Congo states were proclaimed by Congolese political leaders Mar. 12 at the end of a 5-day round-table conference held in Tananarive,

capital of the Malagasy Republic (Madagascar). The agreement was reached by the leaders of the central Congolese
government, Katanga Province and other provincial political groupings. It did not have the support of the rebel Gizenga regime. The conference, presided over by Congolese
Pres. Kasavubu, was convened at the suggestion of Katanga
Pres. Tshombe. Scheduled to begin Mar. 6, it was opened
Mar. 8 after Gizenga, in a statement issued through his
mission to the UAR, said that he considered himself the
legal premier of the Congo and would not go to Tananarive.
The conference ratified the Feb. 28 military alliance concluded by the anti-Gizenga coalition and ordered formation
of a front against "communism in the Congo." It adopted
resolutions pledging each of the Congo's states to respect
neighboring states and to support joint efforts to restore
order in the Congo.

Major provisions of the confederation agreement: (1)
The "ex-Belgian Congo will form a confederation of states
represented on the international plane by a president ... "
(2) A "Council of States"composed of Kasavubu and the
heads of the member states "will determine the general
internal and international policies of the confederation."
(3) "An executive body called the Coordinating Body Between States will carry out the council's decisions." (4)
"The central government will cease to exist when the coordinating body is set up."

A final communique issued by the Congolese leaders in
Tananarive Mar. 12 said that the country's provincial chiefs
would meet to prepare a round-table conference in Elisabethville that would specify the measures to be taken to
"apply the decisions of the present conference."

The conference was attended by Kasavubu, Tshombe,
Premier Ileo of the central government, Albert Kalonji
of South Kasai, Jean Bolikango of Equator, Cleophas Kamitatu of Leopoldville, Joseph Tshomba of Kivu, Barthel-
emy Mukenge of North Kasai and Vital Moanda of the Bakongo district.

At least 2 provincial leaders who did not attend the
Madagascar conference proclaimed independent republics
Mar. 14. Jacques Massa, a member of the Ileo cabinet and
acting premier during Ileo's absence, proclaimed a Main-

dombe State in the north of Leopoldville Province. Jason
Sendwe, an opponent of Tshombe, announced the establishment of a Luluaba State in northern Katanga. A 3d independent state, a Kingdom of the Baluba People, was reported to have been proclaimed in Bakwanga Apr. 9 by
Kalonji. Kalonji, who named himself "king" of the Baluba,
had failed in efforts to found an independent Mining State
in South Kasai in 1960.

In a series of messages transmitted to UN Secy. Gen.
Hammarskjold Mar. 8-14, the Madagascar conferees demanded that the UN Force be curtailed. The first messages,
cabled Mar. 8-9 from Tananarive, demanded that the
UN "abstain from all further action on the Congo pending
the results of this conference." They said much of the
current Congo tension had been caused by UN troops'
actions under the Feb. 21 Security Council resolution
permitting them to use force.

The final communique of the Tananarive meeting announced that the conference had cabled Hammarskjold
and UN Assembly Pres. Frederick Henry Boland to ask
"annulment" of the Feb. 21 resolution on the ground
that it no longer was needed "since reunion has been
achieved."

Gizenga Rejects Agreement

It was reported from Leopoldville Mar. 18 that the
Gizenga government had rejected the confederation agreement. Gizenga was said to have informed Kasavubu that
all decisions adopted by the Tananarive conference were
unacceptable to the Stanleyville government. He was said
to have demanded the reconvening of the Congolese Parliament in a neutral country to seek a new political settlement based on a federation with a strong central government.

Interviewed in Stanleyville Mar. 22 by Marguerite
Higgins of the N.Y. Herald Tribune, Gizenga denied that
he was a Communist but insisted that he was the legal
successor to Lumumba. He said he would expel all Western consular officials from Stanleyville unless their governments recognized him. The consuls were ousted Mar. 24.

UN REPORTS 'CATASTROPHE' NEAR

Hammarskjold Commission's Views

The Congo Conciliation Commission reported Mar. 21 that a 6-week inquiry had shown that the Congo was "on the verge of catastrophe" from civil war, famine, near-bankruptcy, and the threat of foreign intervention. The commission, headed by Jaja Wachuku of Nigeria, circulated the report to the General Assembly and made it public Mar. 21.

The commission's findings: (1) The Congo's "Loi Fondamentale" (constitution) was "incomplete and ill-adapted to the needs of the Congo" and should be replaced or amended. (2) The central Congolese government of Premier Ileo represented a step toward constitutionality, but it "cannot be considered as legal" without Parliamentary approval and should be "broadened without delay . . . to make it a government of national unity." (3) All Congolese military operations "must be halted immediately to avert the . . . danger of civil war." (4) The Congolese army "and the other armed groups now operating in the territory should be insulated from politics and reorganized" under UN guidance, with UN troops assisting Congolese authorities in maintaining order. (5) "A federal form of government can alone preserve the national unity and territorial integrity of the Congolese state," and a "summit meeting" of Congolese leaders should be held to achieve "national reconciliation." (6) In view of recent executions of hostages, all political detainees should be freed immediately. (7) The Congolese Parliament should be reconvened, under UN protection if requested. (8) UN action was necessary to halt "foreign interference in the internal affairs of the Congo" and to force the removal of "Belgian and other foreign military and para-military personnel, political advisers and mercenaries."

The report, written before the Tananarive conference, warned that a further deterioration of the Congo situation would endanger all of Africa.

UN Buildup in Katanga

1,000 Gurkha troops of the Indian UN Force contingent were flown to the Kamina base area Apr. 1-3 to reinforce UN troops attempting to cope with renewed fighting in northern Katanga. The Gurkhas were members of the 4,700-man supplemental Indian troop contribution airlifted to the Congo by U.S. planes in March. The UN buildup followed the Katanga government's announcement Mar. 31 that its troops had retaken Manono, capital of the Luluaba State proclaimed in northern Katanga by Jason Sendwe. The Katanga force, reportedly led by South African mercenaries, routed Sendwe's followers and a force of Gizenga's troops sent into the area in January.

Pres. Tshombe charged Apr. 1 that the arrival of the Indian troops was an "act of war" against his government. Mobs of crudely-armed Katangans attacked Swedish UN troops guarding the Elisabethville airport Apr. 4 after Tshombe had ordered a campaign of popular resistance and sabotage to drive the UN from Katanga.

UN Deals With Fund Crisis

The UN General Assembly voted by 51-10 (22 abstentions) Apr. 3 to approve a 3-week extension of Secy. Gen. Hammarskjold's authority to pay for UN military operations in the Congo. The Assembly empowered Hammarskjold to incur financial commitments for the UN Force until Apr. 21 at the rate of up to $8 million monthly. The resolution was voted despite shouted interruptions by Soviet delegate Aleksei A. Roschin that it violated the UN Charter. (Hammarskjold's authority to commit funds for UN Congo military purposes had expired Mar. 31.) The Assembly voted again April 22 to authorize Hammarskjold to commit up to $10 million monthly for UN Congo activities until the question of financing was settled by the 16th session, scheduled to meet in the fall. The vote, 54-15 (23 abstentions), was on a resolution that granted smaller UN member states reductions of up to 80% in their Congo assessments.

The U.S. informed the UN Apr. 18 that it was prepared to make a $15 million voluntary contribution to the UN treasury in addition to full payment of the $32,510,000 U.S. share of the cost of UN Congo operations through the end of October.

(The N.Y. Times had reported Mar. 28 that France and most Latin American countries had refused to pay their shares of UN special assessments for the Congo operation, $48.5 million in 1960 and an estimated $120 million in 1961. The USSR and Soviet bloc states previously had refused to pay their shares. Only 4 countries— the U.S., Australia, Ireland and the Netherlands—were said to have paid their assessments for 1960 Congo operations. The payments totaled $16,745,329 [$15,745,211 from the U.S.' 32.51% share]; $31,686,574 remained unpaid. UN officials reported Mar. 30 that only $16,881,225 had been contributed to the $100 million Congo Economic Development Fund requested in 1960. $10 million of the amount was contributed by the U.S.)

(An agreement for a $10 million UN loan to the central Congolese government was made public June 12 by Hammarskjold. The financial accord, negotiated by UN Undersecy. Philippe de Seynes and Pres. Kasavubu, provided for reduction of Congolese expenditures on the army and civil service. It called for establishment of a Congo budget that would give priority to health, education and public works. A UN report issued Aug. 12 said that $18 million had been committed from the Congo Economic Development Fund and that the UN civil staff serving in the Congo at UN expense had grown to 750 persons.)

Belgians Again Asked to Leave

A new demand for the withdrawal from the Congo of all Belgian military and political personnel was adopted by the General Assembly Apr. 15 by a 61-5 vote (33 abstentions). The Assembly action came at the end of a 2-week debate on the Congo. Presented by 21 nations, the resolution was shorn of provisions for sanctions if Belgium failed to honor a withdrawal deadline.

Other resolutions on the Congo acted on by the Assembly Apr. 15: (1) A U.S. draft, adopted by 60-16 (23 abstentions), outlining long-range UN aims in the Congo, among them the reconvening of the Congolese Parliament, creation of a broad national government, adoption of a new Congolese constitution and new measures by Hammarskjold to halt delivery of arms to the Congo. (2) A Soviet draft, rejected by 53-29 (17 abstentions), calling for reconvening within 21 days of the Congolese Parliament to settle the crisis stemming from the existence of the rival Gizenga and Kasavubu governments.

A report circulated to the Assembly by Hammarskjold Apr. 15 charged that the Katanga regime was recruiting military personnel in Europe and Africa with the complicity of Belgian officials. Written by Mekki Abbas, deputy UN representative in the Congo, the report was based on the questioning of 30 Katanga mercenaries captured by the UN Force.

Congo Signs UN Force Pact

Pres. Kasavubu Apr. 17 signed a UN agreement accepting the operative provisions of the Feb. 21 Security Council resolution on the Congo. The agreement "recognized" the need for UN-assisted reorganization of the Congolese army and for the expulsion of "all foreign civil officials, military and paramilitary mercenaries and political advisers" not in the service of Leopoldville. The Congolese Army was to be subjected to "discipline and control" to eliminate its "interference ... in the political life of the Congo." The agreement was signed for the UN by Robert K. A. Gardiner of Ghana and Francis C. Nwokedi of Nigeria.

(Congolese Army headquarters in Leopoldville announced Apr. 17 that the commanders of Gizenga's army had signed an agreement submitting their men to the control of Gen. Mobutu, the central government's commander. The agreement was proven to be ineffective by subsequent events. The central government ended a 2-month economic blockade of areas controlled by the Gizenga regime Apr. 18 with the dispatch from Leopoldville of a Congo river barge train carrying 2,000 tons of food.)

TSHOMBE HELD BY LEOPOLDVILLE

Arrested at Coquilhatville Meeting

Katanga Pres. Tshombe was arrested by the central Congolese government in April after he appeared at a conference of Congolese leaders in Coquilhatville, the capital of Equator Province, but walked out of the meeting after rejecting further talks with Pres. Kasavubu's government. Tshombe was held for nearly 2 months. He was freed only after he had pledged to end Katanga's secession and to cooperate in establishing a united Congo. He repudiated his pledge as soon as he returned to Katanga.

The Coquilhatville meeting, convened Apr. 24 by Kasavubu, was a sequel to the Madagascar conference, at which it had been decided to transform the Congo into a confederation of autonomous states. Nearly all major Congolese leaders except Antoine Gizenga attended the meeting. Participants included Tshombe, Premier Ileo and Foreign Min. Bomboko of the central Congolese government, Albert Kalonji of South Kasai, and Jason Sendwe, leader of the separatist regime in northern Katanga. Kasavubu told the conferees Apr. 24 that they were meeting to deal with 5 basic questions: reorganization of the Congolese Army, the structure of a new Congolese state, the Congo's diplomatic representation abroad, relations with the UN and its civil and military commands in Leopoldville, and the country's worsening economic crisis.

Tshombe was arrested by central government troops Apr. 26 after he had walked out of the conference. Tshombe had attacked Kasavubu at the meeting Apr. 24-25 for allegedly betraying the Congo in his relations with the UN. He demanded that the central government renounce its agreement with the UN for reorganization of the Congo's armed forces and expulsion of foreign advisers. He called on the meeting to censure UN Force actions. He led the Katanga delegation from the meeting Apr. 25 and rejected all further discussion unless Kasavubu accepted his demands.

Tshombe, Katanga Foreign Min. Evariste Kimbe and 6 Belgian advisers were arrested by Congolese troops Apr. 26 as they sought to board a plane in Coquilhatville to return to Katanga. Tshombe remained at the airport without food for 2 days while officials sought to persuade him to return to the conference. He was returned to Coquilhatville under arrest Apr. 28. Tshombe was transferred under guard to Leopoldville, where an act of internment filed against him May 9 requested his detention for trial as a "threat to the safety of the state." A similar act was filed against Kimbe May 9, and Tshombe's 6 Belgian aides were deported the same day. The government's legal action against Tshombe was handled by Interior Min. Cyrille Adoula, future premier of the Congo.

(The Katanga government informed Secy. Gen. Hammarskjold May 2 that it was prepared to receive UN representatives to negotiate agreements for reorganizing its armed forces and withdrawing its Belgian advisers. A Katanga cabinet statement issued in Elisabethville called for the immediate release of Tshombe and said his government was ready to cooperate with the UN because the Kasavubu government had accepted Tshombe's demands for creation of a confederation. The Katanga government was said to have come under the control of Interior Min. Godefroid Munongo after Tshombe's arrest. Munongo warned May 6 that Katanga was ready to "fight to the last man" rather than accept Kasavubu's rule. He told an Elisabethville press conference that any effort to impose central government rule would result in "massacres.")

Federal Plan Adopted

The Coquilhatville conference concluded May 28 after adopting a draft constitution providing for the transformation of the Congo into a federal republic of 20 states. The conference also, according to an Apr. 30 announcement by Foreign Min. Bomboko, authorized Kasavubu to take all measures necessary to disarm the separatist armies in Katanga, Oriental, and Kivu.

(Kasavubu had challenged Antoine Gizenga May 13 to agree to the reconvening of the Congolese Parliament and the formation of a unified Congolese government. Gizenga, leader of the Lumumbist government in Stanleyville, rejected the proposal May 16 unless Parliament was convened in Kamina under UN protection. Negotiations for reconvening Parliament were undertaken by the 2 regimes after the Coquilhatville conference and produced an agreement June 19 to hold a Parliamentary session at Lovanium University, outside Leopoldville, in July.)

Tshombe Freed, Repudiates Pledges

An agreement to take steps to end Katanga's secession was forced from Tshombe in June, while he was under detention. Tshombe, released in Leopoldville June 22, appeared at a press conference that day with Premier Ileo and Maj. Gen. Mobutu. He announced that in return for his release he had promised to send Katanga deputies and senators to attend the reconvening of the Congolese Parliament. Tshombe made it clear, however, that he disagreed with the central government on many matters. He stressed his friendship for Mobutu and said he had signed a "military agreement" to integrate Katanga's armed forces with those commanded by Mobutu. The terms of an agreement said to have been signed by Tshombe and Ileo were broadcast by Leopoldville radio June 25. The agreement reportedly provided for central government control of Katanga's army, schools and foreign affairs.

Tshombe returned to Elisabethville by plane June 24 and was given an emotional welcome by Katangans. He publicly repudiated his accord with the central government in a speech to the Katanga Assembly June 28. Tshombe told the Assembly: His arrest had taught him to "work only for Katanga's people" and had proved Katanga capable of self-government in his absence; "we shall defend an independent Katanga and will do everything to maintain our nation in the face of all opposition." Tshombe told newsmen June 29 that Katanga would participate in the reconvening of the Congolese Parliament only if all other

Congolese leaders agreed to meet him to discuss Katanga's terms for the session. The Katanga Assembly July 4 rejected Tshombe's economic, political and military accords with the Ileo government. It ordered Katanga deputies and senators not to participate in the reconvening of the Congolese Parliament.

(Mobutu, who reportedly had been instrumental in arranging Tshombe's release by the central government, went to Elisabethville in mid-July to attempt new negotiations for an end to the Congo's strife. An agreement for the reunification of all Congolese armed forces was signed by Mobutu and Tshombe July 19 but was not carried out.)

GIZENGA ENDS LUMUMBIST REGIME

Accord Reached at Parliament Meeting

The first concrete step toward liquidating Congolese secessionism was taken in August after deputies representing the central government and the Lumumbist regime in Stanleyville met to reconvene the Congolese National Parliament and approve a new central government headed by Cyrille Adoula. Gizenga, whose Stanleyville representatives had been elected to most of Parliament's key posts, agreed to dissolve the Lumumbist movement and to become first vice premier in the Adoula cabinet. (He later repudiated his agreement and returned to Stanleyville, but his efforts to revive the dissident regime were unsuccessful.)

The Congolese Parliament was convened July 27 at Lovanium University, near Leopoldville, under UN Force protection. It was the first time Parliament had met since the Congo's division into 3 warring regions in 1960. The session, opened by Pres. Kasavubu, was attended by more than 200 senators and deputies, including those representing Premier Ileo's central government, and 70 representing Gizenga's Stanleyville regime and his leftist African Solidarity Party. No Katanga representatives attended despite appeals to Tshombe. (Tshombe and Kasavubu met in Brazzaville, capital of the former

French Congo Republic, July 30-31 but failed to agree on terms for Katangan participation in the session.)

Parliamentary officers were elected at an informal meeting held July 25, and the Gizenga delegation won an unexpected victory. Joseph Kasongo, a leader in Gizenga's group, was reelected president of the Chamber of Deputies by 61 votes to 57 for Jacques Massa, a member of Ileo's cabinet. The Chamber's 2 vice presidents and all 4 members of its secretariat were elected from among Gizenga delegates. The Senate presidency was won by Victor Koumoriko, a central government delegate, but the Senate vice presidencies and secretariat posts were all filled by pro-Gizenga senators.

Adoula Cabinet Formed

Cyrille Adoula, 39, a Socialist and interior and defense minister in Ileo's cabinet, was designated Congolese premier Aug. 1 by Kasavubu. He was confirmed as premier Aug. 2 by a nearly unanimous vote in the Chamber (one abstention recorded) and by acclamation in the Senate.

Adoula Aug. 2 presented a national unity cabinet that included Gizenga as first vice premier and Christopher Gbenye, a Gizenga aide, as interior minister. All other posts were said to have been given to followers of the central government. Among them: Justin Bomboko, foreign minister; Joseph Ileo, information minister; Jason Sendwe, 2d vice premier; Jean Bolikango, 3d vice premier. In an inaugural address delivered in Parliament Aug. 3, Adoula declared that his government would reintegrate Katanga within the Congo. He accused Tshombe and Belgian mining interests, among them the Union Miniere du Haut-Katanga, of "a great wrong against the Congo." He declared, however, that the Leopoldville government would recognize regional rights and local autonomy wherever they did not run counter to the national interests of the Congo as a whole. Adoula pledged that his regime would free all political prisoners detained without valid reasons, build a disciplined national army, and accept aid from abroad.

Stanleyville Government Disbanded

The formation of a new central government was followed by the voluntary dissolution of the Stanleyville regime set up by Gizenga and other followers of the late Patrice Lumumba. An announcement to African and Soviet-bloc diplomats in Stanleyville Aug. 5 said that the Gizenga regime had recognized the authority of the Adoula government and would disband. The decision was announced by Marcel Lengema, foreign secretary in the Gizenga cabinet. It was confirmed by Gen. Victor Lundula, commander of the Stanleyville regime's forces.

A public commitment by Gizenga to end his regime and accept the post of first vice premier in the central government cabinet was won by Premier Adoula Aug. 18 at the end of a 3-day visit to Stanleyville. Gizenga, who had informed all foreign diplomats of his decision the previous day, made it clear, however, that "the [Adoula] government will have to follow the Lumumba line, and if ever the government departs from this line . . . I am ready to fight again." Adoula, present when Gizenga spoke, said: "We have achieved what Lumumba wanted—one Congo."

Adoula returned to Leopoldville Aug. 18. He declared that his government would espouse Lumumba's aims—a unified and neutralist Congolese state—and would take concrete steps to end Katanga's secession. (Gizenga did not assume his post in the Adoula cabinet until Sept. 3, when he flew to Leopoldville to accompany Adoula to a Belgrade conference of non-aligned countries.)

Massacres in Kasai, Kivu

Thousands of Congolese were reported killed in tribal warfare in Kasai and Kivu Provinces in June, July and August. The killing of 100 Bashi tribesmen in Nya-Ngezi, near Bukavu, Kivu Province, was reported June 1 by UN Malayan troops in the area. The massacre was attributed to forces of the Stanleyville government, which controlled Kivu Province. UN officials in Elisabethville reported July 19 that hundreds of Kanioka tribesmen had fled marauding soldiers of South Kasai's self-proclaimed

king, Albert Kalonji. Unconfirmed reports said thousands
of tribesmen had been killed and their villages burned
by the Kalonji forces. The massacre of 600 Luntu tribesmen in Kasai was reported by the UN Aug. 2. The Luntu
were said to have provoked the massacre by killing 25
members of a central government patrol that entered
Kasai.

(UN troops had been withdrawn from South Kasai and
all relief operations there halted May 15 after more than
50 UN soldiers had been killed in attacks on their garrison in Port-Francqui. The UN said little could be done
to aid South Kasai in view of "endemic" tribal conflict.)

UN FORCE STRIKES AT KATANGA

Unified Congo Aim of Attack

A UN military attack was launched against the dissident
Katanga regime in mid-September. It was criticized by
many governments as the first instance of military aggression under the UN flag. It was justified by the UN
as necessary to end Katanga's secession and achieve
the goal of a united and viable Congo specified in resolutions approved by an overwhelming majority of UN
member states. The attack was the first of 3 attempts
to suppress by force Katanga's separatism. All ended
short of complete success, and Katanga remained virtually a separate state.

The September attack was due primarily to the continued refusal of Katangan Pres. Tshombe to submit
his regime to the authority of the central Congolese
government and to expel Belgians serving as advisers to
Katanga and as officers in its 13,000-man gendarmerie.
Premier Adoula of the central government had said in
Leopoldville Aug. 19: "I intend to use all means— . . .
force if necessary–to prevent [Katanga's] secession."

The UN began airlifting reinforcements to its 3,000-
man Katanga garrison Aug. 25 to prepare for what UN
officials openly described as a planned attempt to disarm
Tshombe's army and deport its white officers, estimated
to number 500. Conor Cruise O'Brien, the chief UN

representative in Katanga, told reporters Aug. 26 that the UN was prepared to back with force an effort to impose central government authority in Katanga.

Tshombe said at an Elisabethville news conference Aug. 26 that "we are ready to die" rather than negotiate under a UN threat of force.

UN troops Aug. 28 made their first attempt to round up white mercenaries serving Katanga. UN units temporarily seized control of the Elisabethville airport, radio station, post office and military headquarters and arrested nearly 100 whites. Tshombe gave in later Aug. 28 and broadcast orders for the dismissal of all whites from the Katanga gendarmerie and government offices. He refused, however, to enforce the orders despite a 24-hour UN ultimatum delivered Aug. 29. 340 mercenaries were seized and deported by the UN beginning Sept. 1, but many remained. (Many of the most prominent Belgian advisers to Katanga had left the Congo in response to UN pressure. They included: Alexandre Belina, chief political aide to Tshombe, who was arrested with the Katanga delegation in Coquilhatville Apr. 26 and who left the Congo voluntarily; Francis Renard, chief of Katanga police, who left early in June; Col. Guy Weber, Tshombe's military adviser, who agreed to leave June 14; Georges Thyssens, adviser to Katanga; interior Min. Munongo, who was arrested and deported by the UN July 7.)

The UN Command severed relations with the Katanga regime Sept. 1 after Tshombe had rejected UN demands for the ouster of Interior Min. Munongo. The UN had charged Aug. 31 that Munongo was guilty of "organizing atrocities" against refugees from Kasai Province and that he had ordered mercenaries to assassinate UN officials. (Thousands of Baluba tribesmen had sought UN protection in a temporary refugee camp near Elisabethville Aug. 28 after the Katanga regime had arrested 800 on charges of conspiring to strike against the Tshombe government. The arrests were ordered by Munongo. The number of Balubas in the camp grew to more than 30,000 within 2 weeks.) Tension between the UN and the Katanga government grew after the break in relations and was intensified by the outbreak Sept. 6 of Elisabethville riots against UN personnel. Tshombe Sept. 11 announced his rejection of a final UN demand that he begin negotiations with the central government.

International Force Begins Assault

The UN attack was opened in Elisabethville Sept. 13 by Sudanese, Swedish and Irish troops commanded by Indian Brig. K. A. S. Raja. The assault was reported to have been successful. After fighting in which an estimated 50 persons, most of them Katangans, were killed, UN forces reoccupied Elisabethville's post office and radio station. The Elisabethville fighting was accompanied by similar attacks Sept. 13-14 in Jadotville and the Kamina military base area.

The Tshombe regime was declared at an end Sept. 13 by Conor Cruise O'Brien. O'Brien, in a statement issued after UN troops had attacked communications and government buildings in Elisabethville, said: "The secession of Katanga has ended; it now is a Congolese province run by the central government"; the UN attack had been launched "at the request of the central government"; the UN had acted "to avoid the alternative—invasion of Northern Katanga by central government troops and a prolonged civil war."

Tshombe, at first reported to have fled Elisabethville, was discovered and interviewed in the capital Sept. 14 by newsmen. He used the meeting to offer the UN a ceasefire on condition it withdrew from positions seized the previous day and left him free to open talks with the central government.

Katangan counterattacks were launched against the UN positions in Elisabethville Sept. 14-15. Katangan troops making these attacks were said to have been led by whites and cheered by white crowds. They failed to dislodge the UN troops, but they shelled and wrecked most of the UN positions in the capital's center. A Katanga air force jet made several bombing raids Sept. 14-15 on UN headquarters in Elisabethville and positions held by Irish UN soldiers besieged in Jadotville. The 158-man Irish garrison in Jadotville surrendered to Katangan forces Sept.

18. The Katangan military radio claimed the capture of the UN's Kamina base the same day, but news dispatches indicated Sept. 19 that the base remained in the hands of its garrison of 500 Irish and Swedish troops. Katangan troops renewed attacks on UN strongpoints in Elisabethville Sept. 19 but were repelled with heavy loss.

The UN attack in Katanga was supported by the U.S. but was condemned by many UN powers, especially Belgium, Britain and France. A State Department statement Sept. 16 made clear U.S. support for the UN action as legitimate under the Security Council resolution of Feb. 21. The British Foreign Office disclosed Sept. 14 that Britain had expressed its concern directly to Hammarskjold over the UN's use of force in Katanga. Lord Lansdowne, foreign affairs undersecretary, was ordered to meet Hammarskjold in the Congo Sept. 15 to aid in ceasefire talks. The French Foreign Ministry asserted Sept. 15 that UN officials had exceeded their mandate and possibly violated the UN Charter by ordering an "offensive" in the Congo. Moscow radio charged Sept. 15 that Hammarskjold had ordered the attack only to give the illusion of carrying out UN resolutions for the unity of the Congo.

HAMMARSKJOLD KILLED SEEKING TRUCE

Plane Crashes on Way to Talks

UN Secy. Gen. Hammarskjold was killed Sept. 18 when his chartered airliner crashed near Ndola, Northern Rhodesia while carrying him to a meeting with Pres. Tshombe to arrange a truce between Katangan and UN military forces. Hammarskjold had left New York for the Congo Sept. 12, while UN troops were launching their attack on the separatist Katanga regime. He arrived Sept. 13 in Leopoldville, seat of the central Congolese government, and held 3 days of political talks with Premier Adoula and Pres. Kasavubu. These talks ended Sept. 16, and Hammarskjold, who originally had intended to return to New York, decided instead to meet with Tshombe in Ndola to seek an end to the fighting. The

Ndola meeting had been arranged by Lord Lansdowne, British foreign undersecretary.

Hammarskjold left Leopoldville for Ndola Sept. 17 aboard a chartered Swedish DC-6B airliner. (The plane, flown by Capt. Per Hellonquist of Sweden, had been hit on the ground during a strafing attack on Elisabethville airport Sept. 15 by a Katanga jet fighter. A damaged exhaust pipe had been discovered and replaced before the plane left to pick up Hammarskjold.) The 1,100-mile flight from Leopoldville to Ndola should normally have taken the DC-6B 4 hours, but the plane kept radio silence and was believed to have taken a circuitous route to avoid interception by the Katanga jet. Hammarskjold's plane arrived over Ndola after a 6-hour 52-minute flight shortly after midnight the night of Sept. 17-18. It was cleared to land by the Ndola airport control tower but suddenly changed course and disappeared. A search for the missing plane was begun early Sept. 18. The wreckage and the bodies of 13 persons—one of them Hammarsk- jold—were found later Sept. 18 in a forest 6-8 miles north of Ndola airport.

Only one of the 16 persons aboard the plane survived: Harold M. Julian, 36, an American member of the UN security guard. Julian told UN officials the plane had veered away from Ndola on Hammarskjold's instructions. He said the plane had been rocked by explosions and had crashed minutes after changing course. Julian died of burns Sept. 23 in an Ndola hospital without recovering sufficiently to add to his account of the crash. Those killed with Hammarskjold: Heinrich A. Wieschoff, 55, deputy to the UN undersecretary for political and Se- curity Council affairs; Vladimir Fabry, 40, legal adviser to the UN Force in the Congo; William J. Ranallo, 39, Hammarskjold's personal bodyguard and driver; Alice Lalande, UN secretary; Serge Barrau and Francis Eivers, UN guards; Capt. Hellonquist and 5 other crew members, all Swedish. The bodies of 2 Swedish UN soldiers not originally known to be aboard were discovered Sept. 19.

(Hammarskjold's death threw the UN into an organization- al crisis that was only partly resolved by the election Nov. 3 of U Thant of Burma as acting secretary general.)

(The UN General Assembly voted unanimously Oct. 26 to order an inquiry into the causes of the crash. A report transmitted to the UN Dec. 18 by the Federation of Rhodesia and Nyasaland said that its own investigation had "failed to determine any positive causes of the accident.")

Hammarskjold was buried Sept. 29 in Uppsala, Sweden. His state funeral, the first accorded a Swedish commoner since 1900, was attended by King Gustaf VI Adolf and Queen Louise and was conducted by Archbishop Emeritus Erling Eiden, former primate of the Swedish State Lutheran Church. Among world leaders at the funeral: Mongi Slim of Tunisia and Nathan Barnes of Liberia, presidents, respectively, of the UN General Assembly and Security Council; former UN Secy. Gen. Trygve Lie; UN Undersecy. Ralph J. Bunche; Vice Pres. Lyndon Johnson and Amb.-to-UN Stevenson; Premiers Tage Erlander of Sweden and Viggo Kampmann of Denmark.

Cease-Fire Ends Katanga Attack

The truce negotiations that were to have been held by Hammarskjold were opened in Ndola Sept. 19 by Tshombe and Mahmoud Khiari, Tunisian head of UN civil operations in the Congo. A provisional cease-fire accord was made public in Ndola Sept. 20. Principal terms of the agreement: UN and Katanga forces were to retain their current positions and exchange prisoners; neither side was to increase its strength in manpower or in weapons; a 4-man commission was to supervise the cease-fire.

The truce took effect throughout Katanga Sept. 21. Although some minor infractions were reported, the provisional accord generally remained effective. An agreement on a formal UN-Katanga cease-fire was reached in Elisabethville Oct. 13 by Tshombe and Khiari and went into effect with its ratification by the UN Secretariat Oct. 24. With the secretary general's post vacant as a result of Hammarskjold's death, the UN announcement said only that the accord had been "approved by United Nations headquarters." The decision was understood to have been taken by UN Undersecretaries Andrew W. Cordier, Ralph J. Bunche and Chakravarthi V. Narasimhan,

Hammarskjold's Congo military and civil advisers Brig. I. J. Rikhye and Sir Alexander MacFarquhar, and Robert K. Gardiner, UN economic and social affairs aide.

The prisoner exchange and a troop withdrawal started Oct. 25. The UN Force left the radio station and other key points in Elisabethville and accepted Katangan troops in joint occupation of the capital's major airport. 191 UN troops, most of them Irish soldiers captured in Jadotville, were exchanged for 220 Katangans made prisoner by the UN. According to a casualty report issued Sept. 20 by the UN Command in Leopoldville, 20 UN soldiers had been killed and 63 wounded in the Katanga fighting.

The UN-Katanga truce was opposed by the central government. Premier Adoula denounced the accord Oct. 14 for its implied recognition of Katanga and made it clear that he would not be bound by it.

(A decision to form a tactical air force to provide protection for UN Force units in future Congo operations was announced Sept. 22 at UN headquarters in New York. The decision was attributed to the ill-fated night flight that Hammarskjold had been forced to make to avoid interception by Katanga's planes. 4 Ethiopian Air Force F-84 jets, 6 Indian Canberra jet bombers and 6 Swedish Saab jet fighters were sent to the Congo. The U.S., Norway and Denmark announced Sept. 21 that they would send additional transport planes.)

Katanga Routs Congolese Invaders

Troops of the central Congolese government invaded Katanga Province Oct. 30 on orders of Premier Adoula "to liquidate the Katanga secession." The invading forces met strong resistance from Katangan troops and were reported to be in full retreat by Nov. 4.

The invasion was launched despite a UN statement, issued in Leopoldville Oct. 28 by Khiari, that Adoula had committed himself not to send his forces into Katanga. Adoula announced the invasion in a Leopoldville radio speech Oct. 30. He said that "all peaceful means of trying to deal with Tshombe had been used" and his troops had been ordered into Katanga on a "police action" to

restore order "in this region troubled by outlaws." Maj.
Gen. Mobutu said at a Leopoldville news conference Nov.
2 that his forces had invaded Katanga on a wide front
and had advanced up to 35 miles into the dissident province. He asserted that orders for the attack had been
given after prior attacks by Katangan planes. He said
the invaders were being supplied through Kasai.

The central government conceded Nov. 4 that its troops
had been repulsed in an attempt to take the Katanga
military center of Kaniama and were in retreat toward
the Kasai border. Leopoldville spokesmen said that the
invading troops had suffered "heavy losses" near Kaniama, which, they said, was held by elite Katangan
paratroops led by white mercenaries. The central government's rout was said to be complete by Nov. 5. It was
accompanied by a wave of attacks on whites—including
many cases of rape—in Luluabourg by central government soldiers. Order was restored in the city by Nov. 8,
after the marauding Congolese had been disarmed and
many whites had been flown out.

(The 6 Swedish jet fighters donated to the UN Force
after Hammarskjold's death had begun patrols of the
Katanga-Kasai border Oct. 31, simultaneously with the
central Congolese invasion of Katanga. The UN jets were
ordered to shoot down any Katangan planes "identified in
offensive military operations." The UN's announcement
of the patrols declared that they were necessary to protect UN troops in the vicinity of the Congolese-Katangan
fighting. A report transmitted to the Security Council
Nov. 3 by Sture C. Linner charged Katanga with break-
ing its truce with the UN by sending planes on bombing
and strafing attacks deep in Kasai Province. Linner said
the Katanga raids had been carried out Oct. 28-30, before the central Congolese move, and had caused "considerable damage and a number of deaths." A statement
issued Nov. 1 by the State Department declared that the
U.S. "fully supports" UN air action against Katangan planes.
It said the renewed Katanga-Kasai fighting had been "provoked by bomb attacks on the part of aircraft from Katanga."
Tshombe declared Nov. 3 that his planes had bombed only the
Kasai bases used for the Katanga invasion.)

LUMUMBIST MUTINIES BREAK OUT

Gizenga Renews Dissidence

UN officials in the Congo reported Nov. 15 that a wave of mutinies had swept Congolese Army units in Kivu and northern Katanga. The mutineers were believed to be sympathetic to Vice Premier Gizenga and the Lumumbist elements centered in Stanleyville, Oriental Province. Gizenga had left Leopoldville for Stanleyville Oct. 5, ostensibly to take care of personal matters before taking up his post in the central Congolese government. Gizenga, however, overstayed the 8-day time limit on his trip. When he ignored an ultimatum by Premier Adoula to return by Nov. 5 it was conceded that he probably had abandoned his cabinet post to resume leadership of the Stanleyville movement.

Mutinous Congolese troops supporting Gizenga were reported to have seized control of Kindu, in Kivu Province. The Kindu mutineers were said to have invaded the base of the Malayan UN Force garrison Nov. 11 and to have taken prisoner 13 Italian airmen who had flown UN equipment to the city. Other pro-Gizenga mutinies reportedly took place in Luluabourg and in Albertville, a northern Katanga city that had been seized by Baluba tribesmen and occupied by Congolese troops Nov. 14. Indian UN troops in Albertville said the invaders had terrorized the city.

Gizenga, who had gone to Kindu to try to arrange the release of the Italian airmen, openly declared his opposition to the Adoula government Nov. 14. The AP reported from Leopoldville Nov. 15 that he had summoned all former followers of the late Patrice Lumumba to set up a leftwing nationalist political movement.

The UN command in Leopoldville announced Nov. 16 that the 13 Italian airmen had been shot and dismembered Nov. 11 by the Kindu mutineers. The airmen were crew members of 2 C-119 transport planes made available to the UN Force by Italy. They had flown from the Kamina Air Base to Kindu Nov. 11 to deliver scout cars to the

Malayan UN contingent based in Kivu. The UN report on
the slayings, made public by Sture C. Linner, gave the
following account of the murders: The Italians were arrested by Congolese soldiers and were taken to Kindu
Prison, "where they were immediately shot and then
cut to pieces by the soldiers." "Pieces of the bodies
were distributed to the large crowd that had gathered to
watch the massacre. . . . All the remains of the bodies
were then thrown into the river."

Adoula appealed Nov. 16 for UN help against the uprising and the troops responsible for the Italians' slaying.
The Adoula government and UN command announced their
agreement Nov. 17 on a joint commission to probe the
slayings. The UN ordered its Kivu forces Nov. 17 to move
on Kindu and prevent the escape of those responsible for
the massacre. But the UN disclosed Nov. 25 that it had
abandoned efforts to disarm and arrest the Kindu garrison and instead would back the central government in
efforts to administer justice itself.

UN REVIEWS CONGO POLICIES

Council Again Authorizes Force

The UN Security Council met in New York Nov. 13-24
and authorized Acting UN Secy. Gen. U Thant, Hammarskjold's successor, to meet with armed force a new threat
of civil war between the central Congolese government
and Katanga. The Council's view was that if any UN military action was required in the Congo, it should be directed against Katanga.

The Council's decision was embodied in an Asian-African resolution adopted Nov. 24 by a 9-0 vote (Britain and
France abstaining). The resolution reaffirmed prior UN
pledges to defend Congo unity. It deplored "all armed action in opposition to the authority" of the central Congolese government, "specifically, secessionist activities and
armed action" by Katanga. It rejected "the claims that
Katanga is a 'sovereign independent nation.'" The resolution authorized Thant "to take vigorous action, including
the use of requisite measures of force, for the immediate

. . . deportation of all foreign military and paramilitary personnel and political advisers" not under the UN command. It authorized UN measures to prevent the further entry of arms or personnel for the Katanga provincial government.

Soviet Deputy Foreign Min. Valerian A. Zorin cast the USSR's 96th and 97th Security Council vetoes to prevent the adoption of key amendments proposed by U.S. Amb.-to-UN Stevenson. These were (1) a request that Thant help reorganize and retrain the Congolese army, and (2) a draft deploring all armed attacks on forces of the UN and the central Congolese government. Stevenson said Nov. 24 that the U.S. had voted for the Asian-African resolution "with the greatest reluctance" to make clear it supported the central government in its battle against Katanga.

Thant, in a statement to the Council after the vote, promised to carry out the resolution "with determination and vigor." He said later that the earlier Council resolutions on the Congo gave him the authority to attempt a reorganization of the Congolese army and a reconciliation of the Congo's warring factions despite the defeat of the U.S. amendments.

Tshombe Challenges UN

Pres. Tshombe warned the UN Nov. 25 that any attempt to suppress his regime would be resisted "even if the whole Katanga population—black and white—had to die." Tshombe made the declaration at an Elisabethville press conference called specifically to reply to the Security Council resolution. He said Katanga was ready "for any negotiation and solution of the problem," but "if we are attacked, we will reply with force." Tshombe, in cables to U Thant and the Security Council, had offered Nov. 17 to begin "immediate negotiations" with the Adoula government. His conditions were that Katanga be recognized as "a sovereign and independent nation" and that the UN intervene to halt any invasions of Katanga. He said he would negotiate only on the basis of the Tananarive agreement, reached in March, for the creation of a Congolese confederation. His terms were rejected by Congolese Foreign Min. Bomboko in New York Nov. 17.

The UN-Katanga truce was further strained by a series of attacks on key UN personnel and troops stationed in and around Elisabethville. Katangan authorities ignored repeated UN demands for a halt to the attacks.

The first serious incident occurred Nov. 28 when marauding Katangan troops assaulted the UN's 2 leading officials in Katanga, George Ivan Smith and Brian Urquhart. The 2 were seized and beaten while they attended a dinner in Elisabethville in honor of visiting U.S. Sen. Thomas J. Dodd (D., Conn.). 2 Indian soldiers serving with the UN Force were kidnaped by Katangans Nov. 28; one of them was found shot to death near Tshombe's Elisabethville home Nov. 29. 32 drunken Katangan soldiers were captured and disarmed by Indian UN troops Dec. 2 after they had fired on the Indians at Elisabethville airport. Katangan forces retaliated Dec. 3 by firing on several UN planes. At least 14 UN officials were kidnaped from their Elisabethville homes Dec. 2-3 by Katangan soldiers.

The UN announced Dec. 3 that Thant had ordered UN representatives in the Congo to "act vigorously to reestablish law and order and protect life and property in Katanga."

NEW UN ATTACK LAUNCHED IN KATANGA

Limited Victory Reported

Heavy fighting broke out in the Elisabethville area Dec. 5 between UN and Katangan forces. The fighting was the result of a UN attack said to have been ordered by Acting Secy. Gen. Thant. The UN attack failed to destroy the Katanga regime. It attained a limited victory, however, in that UN troops were in control of most key Katangan military and administrative centers before the fighting ended Dec. 18.

UN spokesmen in New York said Dec. 5 that UN troops had attacked Katangan roadblocks erected near Elisabethville in violation of the truce agreement. The attack was launched after Thant cabled Sture C. Linner, UN Congo operations chief, to order military action if Katanga ignored demands for removal of the roadblocks and cessation of attacks on UN personnel. The UN spokesmen said that the attack was launched after the roadblocks were strengthened and "it became apparent that Katangese forces intended to launch an attack on the United Nations at the [Elisabethville] airport." The Katangan roadblocks had been erected Dec. 3; Katanga Foreign Min. Evariste Kimba had agreed to their removal within 24 hours, but his promise was not kept.

Tshombe charged Dec. 5 in Paris that the UN had begun the new attack and that Katanga would resist the "aggression." (Tshombe had left Elisabethville Dec. 1, en route to Brazil to attend a conference of the Moral Re-Armament movement.) Tshombe's cabinet held an emergency session in Elisabethville Dec. 5, and Kimba said at a news conference that Katanga considered itself at war with the UN. Tshombe returned to Elisabethville Dec. 8.

The UN's 6,000 men in Katanga were commanded by Indian Brig. K. A. S. Raja, who was named Dec. 5 to head all UN operations in the province. The garrison was backed by a UN air force of 15 modern jet fighters. Additional reinforcements, principally 250 Swedish troops and 700 Ethiopians, were flown to Katanga by U.S. Air Force Globemasters made available to the UN for missions within the Congo for the first time. The UN's forces faced an estimated 12,000 Katangan soldiers and gendarmes, many of them in units commanded by white mercenaries. Katanga was known to have 2 jets and 20 civil aircraft. One of the jets was destroyed Dec. 6 in a UN raid on Kolwezi airport.

Summary of the Katanga fighting:

Dec. 5—The first shots were fired when Indian UN troops tried to force the Katangan roadblock cutting the Elisabethville airport off from the city. The firing spread to other parts of Elisabethville. Crowds panicked in the central business section when Katangans led by mercenaries began shelling UN headquarters.

Dec. 6—Swedish troops attacked and captured a key road underpass and the refugee camp for Baluba tribesmen near the capital. (About 40,000 Baluba were in the camp.) UN jets, flying their first combat missions, raided Kolwezi and highways outside Elisabethville.

Dec. 7-8—Fighting continued in the city's center and near the airport. UN troops were accused of shelling the Prince Leopold Hospital and causing the deaths of 7 Africans. UN jets destroyed a munitions dump near Elisabethville.

Dec. 9-10—UN jets made their first attacks on downtown Elisabethville; they strafed the post office and radio station and raided and burned Camp Massart, the principal military installation in the city. Other air attacks were reported on Union Miniere fuel dumps and transport facilities in Kolwezi.

Dec. 11-12—Katangan mortar attacks were reported against the airport and UN headquarters. UN air raids were directed against Jadotville and Luena.

Dec. 13-14—UN jets attacked and partly destroyed Elisabethville's Lido Hotel, occupied by Katangan forces. A UN-Katangan mortar duel destroyed many homes. (Newsmen reported that UN shells had fallen on the Prince Leopold Hospital and on another hospital in Shinkolobwe, near Elisabethville.)

Dec. 15-16—UN troops, led by Gurkhas, launched their major attack toward Elisabethville's center and reached within 350 yards of the business district. Swedish troops took Camp Massart, and Ethiopian units reached the Lido Hotel area. As they neared Elisabethville's center, the UN troops were reported to have come under heavy sniper fire from white civilians.

Dec. 17-18—5,000 UN troops made a final assault on downtown Elisabethville. They attacked the radio station, railway terminal, Presidential palace and other key objectives but failed to dislodge Katangans and mercenaries from all of them. Union Miniere headquarters was strafed and burned, and the refugee-filled Leopold II Hotel was shelled. UN armored patrols controlled the streets but Katangans continued to occupy many strongpoints in the heart of the city.

Cease-Fire Ordered by UN

UN forces in Katanga were ordered by U Thant to begin a temporary cease-fire Dec. 18. 2 primary conditions were attached to the UN order: (1) that UN forces achieve their "immediate objectives" in the Elisabethville area, and (2) that "firm arrangements" be made for Katanga Pres. Tshombe to fly to the UN-controlled Kitona Air Base for talks with Premier Adoula of the central government. If the conditions were met, UN forces were to hold fire throughout Katanga, unless attacked, for the duration of the Kitona talks.

The Elisabethville fighting was suspended Dec. 18, when Katangan Information Min. Albert Nyembo announced that Tshombe had accepted Thant's conditions. Brig. Raja issued orders for a "hold-fire" later in the day. Conditions remained quiet in the city except for an attack on the Union Miniere headquarters Dec. 19 by Ethiopian troops after they had come under sniper fire from the buildings. (The UN reported Jan. 20, 1962 that the December Katanga fighting took the lives of 200 Katangans, 6 white "mercenaries" and 21 UN troops. The UN listed 50 African civilians wounded in the action.)

WESTERN RIFT OVER FIGHTING

Thant Defends UN Position

The UN military offensive against the Katanga regime divided the Western powers, especially after it became an apparent full-scale effort to suppress Tshombe's government. The UN action was supported by the Kennedy Administration despite some strong Congressional opposition, both Democratic and Republican. It was supported also by Canada, a few smaller European states, and India and other key members of the Asian-African blocs. There were indications of backing from the USSR, which refrained from attacks on UN Congo policies during the fighting. It was strongly opposed, however, by Britain, France, Belgium and other European countries with interests in Africa.

The UN action in Katanga was defended by Thant from its inception as necessary to restore order in the province and carry out the Congo resolutions approved by a large majority of UN member states. In a statement Dec. 10 at UN headquarters in New York, Thant denied that UN operations in Katanga were designed "to force a political solution of the Katanga problem by smashing the political strength of the present political leadership there, as also the leadership itself." He said the UN had acted only after its troops had been the target of Katangan attacks, "which were clearly part of a plan." He declared that the UN would stop fighting only after its security had been restored and it was able to "go ahead with the implementation of the Security Council and General Assembly resolutions" calling for the departure of mercenaries from Katanga and safeguarding of the Congo's territorial integrity.

Thant refused to act on a British request Dec. 13 for a truce on the ground that the Katanga regime had shown no interest in halting the fighting. He told his 19-nation Advisory Committee on the Congo Dec. 16 that the imposition of a cease-fire before UN troops had taken their "short-term objectives" "would be a serious setback" for the UN. He agreed to the Dec. 18 cease-fire only after UN troops had penetrated the center of Elisabethville and the Tshombe government had committed itself to unity talks.

U.S. Backs Attack on Katanga

U.S. support for the UN action in Katanga was made clear by Amb.-to-UN Stevenson Dec. 6 after a personal meeting with Thant. Stevenson said: "The United States is very pleased with the plans of the secretary to bring Katanga under control." The U.S. stand was reiterated in statements made by State Secy. Dean Rusk and Acting State Secy. George W. Ball. Rusk, addressing a news conference Dec. 8, said: "I should like to reiterate United States support for the current program of Secy. Gen. U Thant to restore freedom of movement for United Nations forces in Katanga." Rusk said "the UN must not be prevented from fulfilling its mandate." Ball said at a news conference Dec. 13: "We want a cease-fire as soon as feasible. But we do not believe any cease-fire is feasible until the minimum objectives of the UN have been attained. There cannot be a repetition of the events of September when the United Nations was widely regarded as having suffered a defeat at the hands of the Katanga authorities."

The State Department announced Dec. 6 that the U.S. had made available to the UN 21 more Air Force transports to fly men and supplies to UN troops in Katanga. The U.S. already had contributed 6 C–124 Globemasters for UN Congo operations. Katanga Pres. Tshombe, leaving Paris to return to Katanga Dec. 7, charged that U.S. planes disguised with UN markings had "bombed and killed Negro women and children" in Katanga. The U.S., he asserted, "finds it completely normal to . . . kill little Negroes in Katanga to give pleasure to Communist friends in the UN." Tshombe reiterated his charges when he reached Elisabethville Dec. 8. He said: The U.S. was emulating the USSR's suppression of the 1956 Hungarian revolt; "the American are sending dollars, planes and diplomats to the Congo, everything except soldiers because the American man is too cowardly . . . to carry out such dangerous tasks as long as he can use the skin and the blood of the men of Mr. Nehru, " an allusion to the UN troops supplied by India.

Pres. Kennedy intervened personally in the crisis Dec. 14 after receiving a message in which Tshombe affirmed his willingness to open talks with the central government and appealed to Mr. Kennedy "to stop at once . . . useless bloodshed." The President communicated with both Tshombe and Premier Adoula Dec. 14 and designated U.S. Amb.-to-Congo Edmund A. Gullion as his personal representative in efforts to bring the 2 Congolese leaders together. Informed by Gullion Dec. 17 that Adoula had agreed to meet with Tshombe, Mr. Kennedy cabled the Katanga leader the same day to assure him that Gullion would accompany him to the meeting and would guarantee his safety against a repetition of his arrest at the Coquilhatville conference.

The Kennedy Administration's position came under political attack Dec. 19. Ex-Vice Pres. Nixon, in a syndicated article in the N.Y. Herald Tribune, charged that U.S. policy toward the Congo had been a failure and that, with the support of UN neutralists, it was leading toward a Communist takeover of the Congo. Nixon described Tshombe as a dedicated anti-Communist and the Adoula government as Communist-infiltrated. Sen. Thomas J. Dodd (D., Conn.) charged UN troops with "naked aggression" and "atrocities" against Katanga and demanded a Senate probe of the U.S.' Congo policy. (Dodd's statement was endorsed Dec. 30 by ex-Pres. Herbert Hoover.) Similar views had been expressed by Sens. Barry Goldwater (R., Ariz.), James O. Eastland (D., Miss.) and Richard B. Russell (D., Ga.), and by Senate GOP leader Everett M. Dirksen (Ill.). (Dirksen was listed among 81 sponsors of a private American Committee for Aid to Katanga Freedom Fighters formed Dec. 14, but he denied authorizing use of his name by the group. The committee was headed by Max Yergan, a Negro educator.)

The Administration's policies were defeated in a speech made by State Undersecy. Ball Dec. 19 and at an executive meeting held with State Secy. Rusk Dec. 20 by the Senate Foreign Relations Committee. Ball said: UN intervention in the Congo had been "the only alternative to big-power intervention"; "if one looks at the problem from the viewpoint of saving all of Central Africa from chaos and Communist infiltration, then clearly the acceptance of armed secession by a tribal area . . . can lead only to disaster"; the UN's armed action "was necessary to prevent a civil war."

British, French, Belgian Opposition

British and French opposition to the U.S. stand was made clear to State Secy. Rusk Dec. 10 in Paris by British Foreign Secy. Lord Home and French Foreign Min. Maurice Couve de Murville. The 3, meeting in advance of a NATO Ministerial Council session, were able to agree only that there should be "a united and peaceful Congo." The British and French position was backed by

Belgium and most of the other NATO ministers at their Council session Dec. 12.

Britain's position had been defended Dec. 6 by Edward Heath, Lord Privy Seal and foreign affairs spokesman in the House of Commons. Heath told Parliament that "the UN forces are of course fully entitled to protect themselves when they are attacked, but they have not got a permit from the resolutions to try to impose a political solution by force." Lord Home told the House of Lords Dec. 7 that Britain was opposed to "force . . . being carried to a point of leading the United Nations into an endless war and chaos." A British decision to supply 24 1,000-pound bombs for use by the UN's Indian Canberra jets was confirmed Dec. 8 but was made subject to political conditions Dec. 11 after strong Conservative opposition. The UN withdrew its request for the bombs Dec. 13.

Belgian Foreign Min. Paul-Henri Spaak charged in 2 messages to Thant Dec. 8 that UN forces had begun "war operations" against Katanga and had caused widespread damage to property and loss of life among the province's civilians. Thant replied Dec. 8, rejecting Belgian charges of UN aggression and brutality. He accused Belgium's Union Miniere interests of supporting and financing Katangan resistance to integration in the Congo. He warned that the UN might have to act against the firm's Congo installations unless it ceased such aid. A statement issued by the company Dec. 9 denied Thant's charges.

A French Foreign Ministry statement declared Dec. 8 that France maintained "complete reserve" toward UN actions in Katanga. It described them as contrary to the UN Charter. France closed its airspace Dec. 15 to planes carrying men or supplies to the UN forces in Katanga.

A British aide-memoire transmitted to U Thant Dec. 13 called on him to "secure an immediate cease-fire in Katanga" and facilitate a negotiated settlement. It was ignored by Thant. Lord Home warned in the House of Lords Dec. 18 that the UN, if it persisted in its Congo actions, might "sow the seeds of its own destruction." He asserted that "matters could come to such a pass that we should have to withdraw our support" for the

UN. In an address Dec. 28 to a British UN Association branch in Berwick-Upon-Tweed, Home said: The UN had reached a point where "a large part of the organization which is dedicated to peace openly condones aggression"; "the chaos in the Congo" was the result of premature independence and of "reckless" UN resolutions against colonialism.

(Charges that Britain and France deliberately had sabotaged UN operations in Katanga were made by Conor Cruise O'Brien, UN representative in Katanga, following his release from the UN post Dec. 1 and his resignation from the Irish Foreign Service Dec. 2. O'Brien, in a statement distributed at UN headquarters Dec. 2, said he had quit his posts to regain "freedom of speech" on events in Katanga. He charged that Britain and France had "bitterly" opposed implementing UN resolutions on Katanga and had used "heavy pressure" to end his efforts to carry them out. He charged that the British UN delegation was "not particularly fastidious about the methods it employed" against him. In a 2d statement issued Dec. 4, O'Brien specifically accused Prime Min. Macmillan and others of "sabotaging" the UN by working for the secession of Katanga.)

KATANGA SIGNS UNITY PACT

Tshombe Hedges on Declaration

An agreement to submit Katanga to the authority of the central Congolese government was negotiated by Pres. Tshombe and Premier Adoula in meetings Dec. 20-21 at the UN-held Kitona air base, southwest of Leopoldville. But the accord was partially repudiated by Tshombe as soon as he returned to Elisabethville.

The Kitona accord consisted of an 8-point declaration in which Tshombe recognized the authority of the Congo's Fundamental Law (provisional constitution) and a letter in which he asserted that he would seek authorization by "the competent authorities of Katanga" to implement the declaration. The negotiations, opened by Tshombe and Adoula Dec. 20, broke down late the first day but were resumed after the intervention of UN Undersecy. Ralph J. Bunche and U.S. Amb.-to-Congo Edmund A. Gullion. The Tshombe declaration, as reported by U Thant in a message to the Security Council Dec. 22: "The president . . . of Katanga: (1) Accepts the application of the Fundamental Law of May 19, 1960. (2) Recognizes the indissoluble unity of the Republic of the Congo. (3) Recognizes Pres. Kasavubu as head of state. (4) Recognizes the authority of the central government over all parts of the republic. (5) Agrees to the participation of representatives of the Province of Katanga in the Governmental Commission to be convened at Leopoldville on Jan. 3, 1962 with a view of the draft constitution. (6) Pledges himself to take all necessary steps to enable deputies and senators of the Province of Katanga to discharge, from Dec. 27, 1961, their national mandate within the government of the republic. (7) Agrees to the placing of the Katanga gendarmerie under the authority of the president of the republic. (8) Pledges himself to ensure respect for the resolutions of the General Assembly and the Security Council and to facilitate their implementation."

Despite his declaration, Tshombe, in a statement issued on his return to Elisabethville Dec. 21, asserted that the Kitona accord could take effect only after ratification by Katanga's cabinet and parliament. Declaring that he had "not found anything" in the Kitona talks, Tshombe said: "The important thing is that the accord we have reached has to be ratified by my ministers and by the National Assembly of Katanga." A Katanga cabinet communique issued in Elisabethville Dec. 22 said that the Kitona agreement had been "imposed" on Tshombe and could not become effective unless ratified by the Katanga Assembly. It "congratulated Tshombe . . . for avoiding committing the Katangan people without their previous assent."

Despite the Katangan disavowals of the Kitona agreement, 6 Katangan members of Parliament, 3 deputies and 3 senators, flew to Leopoldville Dec. 27 and took their seats in Parliament Dec. 28. Tshombe said they had been sent to negotiate a revision of the Congo's constitution to permit Katanga continued autonomy.

(The Congolese Parliament had voted unanimously Nov. 27 to resume diplomatic relations with Belgium and the 2 countries announced the resumption of ties Dec. 27. Diplomatic relations with the USSR, Poland and Czechoslovakia, suspended in 1960, were resumed by the Congolese government Dec. 3. Parliament voted Dec. 16 to dissolve the regime of Albert Kalonji, self-proclaimed king of an independent South Kasai state. Kalonji's parliamentary immunity was ended Dec. 28, and he was arrested in Leopoldville Dec. 30.)

(U Thant called on Britain Dec. 29 to permit the stationing of UN observers in Northern Rhodesia to prevent the smuggling of arms and supplies into Katanga from the Federation of Rhodesia and Nyasaland. UN officials in the Congo had reported Dec. 26 that substantial military aid had been provided for Katanga by the federation. They said that a Katanga-owned Dornier bomber had operated from Ndola, Northern Rhodesia, and that 30 Rhodesians had been seen in Kipushi, near Elisabethville, with mobile heavy mortars. The UN had charged Dec. 23 that 48 armed jeeps, driven by Europeans and equipped with machineguns, had crossed into Katanga from Northern Rhodesia Dec. 21. The UN charges were denied Dec. 26 by Sir Roy Welensky, prime minister of the Rhodesia-Nyasaland federation.)

Union Miniere Accused

UN and U.S. officials charged Dec. 27-28 that the Belgian-run Union Miniere du Haut-Katanga had actively abetted Katanga's fight against the UN and was indirectly responsible for political attacks on UN Congo policy. A report by Sture C. Linner, made public by the UN Dec. 28, asserted that during the Elisabethville fighting, attacks had been made on UN forces by "a hard core of non-African extremists and mercenaries" operating from Union Miniere facilities. It said that when UN troops captured the firm's buildings in the city, it found an anti-aircraft gun, ammunition and other military facilities on the property. The UN earlier had charged that the firm's workshops had armed Katanga's planes.

The U.S. accusations were made in addresses delivered Dec. 27 by Asst. State Secy. G. Mennen Williams in Detroit and by Deputy Asst. State Secy. Carl T. Rowan in Philadelphia. They alleged that European and American opposition to UN Congo policies had been instigated by a Katanga propaganda campaign financed by Union Miniere. Rowan said: "Union Miniere pays about 80% of the tax revenues of Katanga and . . . would rather see Katanga as an easily-controlled 'separate nation' than as part of a larger Congo nation whose government might not be as friendly as Mr. Tshombe." Both speeches named Michel Struelens, chief of the Katanga Information Service in New York, as the propaganda chief in the U.S.

Union Miniere had been formed in 1906 to exploit Katanga's huge copper reserves. The firm produced an estimated 60% of the world's cobalt and 8.4% of its copper. It employed 1,700 whites and 22,000 Africans. It controlled concessions totaling 7,700 square miles, nearly the area of New Jersey. The firm's assets were valued at $2½ billion in 1960, before Congolese unrest brought a drop in value of its shares from approximately $1,000 to $220. 18.14% of Union Miniere's stock was held in trust for the Congo; 14.47% was held by Tanganyika Concessions, Ltd. (Britain's Rhodes interests); 13.11% was held by Belgian interests (4.64% by the Societe Generale investment trust, and 8.77% by the Compagnie du Katanga, both of which were said to own a substantial part of Tanganyika Concessions); 53.98% was held by 120,000 shareholders, 25% of them French. According to the Dec. 12 N.Y. Times, Union Miniere spokesmen in Brussels estimated the firm's payments to the Katanga government at approximately $52 million in 1961. This included taxes, franchise payments and dividends on the stock held in trust for the Congo as a whole. The Katanga government had made the dividend payments a condition for uninterrupted Union Miniere production.

1962

Katanga Province refused at the beginning of 1962 to implement its agreement to reunite with the rest of the Congo under the central government in Leopoldville. Katangan Pres. Tshombe began lengthy negotiations with Premier Adoula, but the two leaders again failed to agree on the terms for Katangan reintegration. A UN plan for the imposition of international trade and economic sanctions against the dissident province did not obtain necessary international support, and the world organization again moved toward a military solution of the problem of Katangan separatism. At the year's end, UN troops launched a major offensive against the Katanga regime and appeared to have inflicted a decisive defeat on it.

SECESSION PROBLEM REMAINS

Katanga Scene of New Fighting

Katanga Pres. Moise Tshombe charged Jan. 1 in Elisabethville that 13,000 central government troops had crossed into northern Katanga and were advancing on Kongolo. The central government forces took Kongolo the same day. Tshombe accused the central Congolese force of killing hundreds of Katangans and burning villages in the path of the invasion. He said that Katangan troops had abandoned Kongolo but had held Kapona after repelling with heavy casualties an attack by the invaders. Tshombe said the attack on Kongolo had been launched from Kivu Province with UN air support, but UN spokesmen denied the charge. Tshombe said Jan. 21 that Leopoldville's troops had invaded central Katanga, reaching Kiluva, 250 miles north of Elisabethville.

The murders of 19 Belgian Roman Catholic missionaries and 3 laymen by marauding Congolese soldiers in Kongolo were reported in dispatches from the Congo Jan. 17. According to UN headquarters officials in Leopoldville and to accounts given by the Catholic news agency DAI, the priests were beaten and shot Jan. 1 and their bodies mutilated and thrown into a nearby river. The murders reportedly were witnessed by 50 African student priests. Similar massacres of nuns, priests, other missionaries, European laymen and Africans were reported in the Kongolo area and in Kivu Province throughout January. Pope John XXIII expressed sorrow at the slayings Jan. 17 but said no true Christian would feel hatred—even against the murderers.

Sture C. Linner, Swedish head of UN operations in the Congo, said Jan. 26 that Tshombe apparently was trying to comply with UN and Congolese demands for the dismissal of white mercenaries from Katanga's service. Tshombe appealed Jan. 27 for a month's time in which to track down and expel foreign mercenaries. The Katangan appeal for time was rejected by the UN Jan. 29.

Linner, in a report made public that day, lauded Tshombe's willingness to cooperate in ridding Katanga of the mercenaries but declared that Katanga's commitments specified that this be accomplished "without delay." UN officials in New York disclosed Feb. 5 that Tshombe had agreed to the jointly supervised removal of mercenaries from Katanga.

(Acting UN Secy. Gen. U Thant announced Jan. 26 that Linner had asked to resign as chief of UN operations in the Congo and would be replaced temporarily by Robert K. A. Gardiner of Ghana. Gardiner, who had left Ghana in 1959 to protest politicization of its civil service, was to hold the rank of UN undersecretary.)

A renewal of fighting in northern Katanga was reported Feb. 17. The clashes were centered in the vicinity of Kongolo and Albertville, the province's port on Lake Tanganyika. Kongolo was attacked and recaptured by Katanga forces Feb. 17 after the occupying central government troops had been weakened by withdrawals. The withdrawals had been ordered by Leopoldville after the massacre of Roman Catholic priests. A UN statement, issued in Leopoldville Feb. 23, denounced the Katanga troop movements and demanded that UN forces be permitted to enter and occupy Kongolo. Gardiner declared Feb. 26 at a Leopoldville news conference, however, that no Katangan forces were in action in northern Katanga and that the UN would not help the central government with its plan to airlift 2,000 troops into the disputed area. Gardiner said that Kongolo had been taken by Katangan forces without incident after the city's garrison had deserted.

Central Government Holds Gizenga

The Congolese National Parliament Jan. 8 ordered leftist Deputy Premier Antoine Gizenga to return to Leopoldville from his Stanleyville, Oriental Province stronghold and stand trial for leading a secession movement against the central regime of Premier Cyrille Adoula. Gizenga was the heir to the following of the late Premier Patrice Lumumba.

The resolution was presented by members of Gizenga's own African Solidarity Party; it was supported by a statement in which Premier Adoula cited Gizenga's refusal to heed repeated orders to return to Leopoldville and assume his cabinet duties. ASP Vice Pres. Felicien Kimvay announced Jan. 9 that Gizenga had been ousted from the party for his disloyalty both to the ASP and the central government. (But a rival ASP faction announced later Jan. 9 that an anti-Gizenga group, including Kimvay and Cleophas Kamitatu, themselves had been ousted from the party.) Gizenga was censured by Parliament and was dismissed as deputy premier Jan. 15. The Parliamentary motion, approved by a vote of 67 to one (4 abstentions), censured Gizenga for his refusal to heed Parliament's demand that he return to face secession charges.

Fighting broke out in Stanleyville Jan. 13 between central government troops and an estimated 300 pro-Gizenga soldiers and gendarmes. Most of Gizenga's forces surrendered by Jan. 14, and Gizenga became a prisoner of a mixed force of Congolese troops and of Ethiopian soldiers of the UN command. Gizenga was flown to Leopoldville by the UN Jan. 20 and was handed over to the central government.

Adoula in U.S. Political Talks

Premier Adoula visited the U.S. early in February for talks with UN officials and Pres. Kennedy. Arriving in New York by plane Feb. 2, Adoula addressed the UN General Assembly the same day and appealed for increased UN military assistance to suppress the Katangan secession and to enforce UN resolutions calling for a unified and independent Congo. Adoula said: "Our first concern is the re-establishment of national unity"; the central Congolese government would oppose with force continuation of the Katangan secession or "any other attempt to divide us"; the Katangan rebellion was due to "an unleashed gendarmerie and a handful of greedy mercenaries who wish to take out on the Congolese people their failure in other parts of Africa." African and Soviet-bloc delegates applauded when he called the late Patrice

Lumumba "our national hero."

After conferences in New York with UN officials and representatives of various governments, Adoula flew to Washington, where he conferred with Mr. Kennedy and lunched at the White House as the President's guest. U.S. officials said Mr. Kennedy had assured Adoula of continued U.S. support through the U.N. for his efforts to unify the Congo. Adoula returned to New York and conferred with U Thant Feb. 6. He said at a meeting of the UN Correspondents Association Feb. 7 that he opposed renewed UN military action against Katanga until Pres. Tshombe had been given a chance to carry out his pledge to cooperate with the UN on the mercenary problem and with the central government on the Congo's political reunification.

CONGO UNITY ACCORD IN DOUBT

Katanga Fails to Ratify Pact

The Congolese unity agreement signed in Kitona Dec. 20, 1961 by Pres. Tshombe and Premier Adoula remained a dead letter at the beginning of 1962. Tshombe, who had pledged in Kitona that he would seek rapid ratification of the agreement, told a special session of the Katanga National Assembly in Elisabethville Jan. 4 that only 6 of the 8 points covered by the agreement were acceptable to the Katanga government. The 2 points rejected by Tshombe were those most basic to the agreement: Katanga's acceptance of the Congo's Fundamental Law (provisional constitution), and its implementation of UN resolutions calling for the expulsion of all mercenaries serving in the province's government and armed forces. Tshombe declared that Katanga could carry out these 2 points only after the UN and the central government had proved their good faith.

The Kitona accords were approved by the Katanga Assembly Feb. 15 after an intermittent 6-week debate during which fresh clashes occurred in northern Katanga between forces of Katanga, the central government and the UN Command. The Assembly ratified the Kitona ac-

cords as negotiated but appended to its ratification these
conditions: (1) an end of military operations against Katanga by either UN or central Congolese forces; (2)
adequate Katangan representation in the central Congolese cabinet; (3) amendment of the Congolese constitution
to establish a federal system in which the central government's powers would be limited to foreign affairs, defense,
monetary matters and economic coordination; (4) the withdrawal from Katanga of Ethiopian UN units accused of
atrocities against the Katangan population; (5) central
government pledges to take action against communism
and "certain imperialist countries."

Tshombe-Adoula Talks Indecisive

Tshombe and Adoula held 2 lengthy conferences in
Leopoldville Mar. 18-Apr. 17 and May 18-June 26 but
failed to reach any settlement of their governments'
political differences. Tshombe arrived in Leopoldville under UN protection Mar. 15 to begin the talks but was
forced to wait 3 days in his UN-guarded residence while
Adoula made a trip outside the capital in an obvious effort to snub the Katangan.

The 2 leaders began their talks, closed to newsmen
and all but a few aides, at Adoula's home Mar. 18. They
met daily until Mar. 24, when the meetings were said to
have been suspended due to Tshombe's insistence that
any agreement be submitted to the Katanga Assembly.
Adoula charged in a personal communique Mar. 27 that
Tshombe had "completely ignored the Fundamental Law
and his agreement at Kitona." Tshombe denied the charge
and reiterated in a Mar. 28 communique that Katanga
was ready to accept a reasonable settlement based on
provincial autonomy. Adoula retorted Mar. 29 that Tshombe was delaying a decision "to gain time to improve his
military status." The 2 leaders met again a few times
early in April, but the first phase of their negotiations
was broken off without result Apr. 17 when Adoula again
left Leopoldville.

Tshombe was detained at Leopoldville's Ndjili Airport
for 16 hours Apr. 18-19 when he sought to fly to Katanga

aboard a UN-chartered airliner. Take-off was blocked by fire trucks on central government orders. The trucks were removed after UN Undersecy. Robert K. A. Gardiner protested to the central government and ordered UN troops to use force if necessary to clear the runway for Tshombe's plane.

Tshombe returned to Leopoldville May 18, and resumed his negotiations with Adoula May 22. In this 2d phase of their negotiations, the 2 leaders were joined by Gardiner. Tshombe and Adoula said in a joint communique May 30 that they had reached an accord on integrating Katanga's armed forces into the Congolese army under the auspices of the UN. The accord provided for a joint military commission to work out arrangements for the measure under the chairmanship of a UN officer.

The talks were interrupted at several points early in June by a growing dispute over the basic issue: Katanga's demand for self-government in a Congolese federation. Tshombe, in his first personal statement since returning to Leopoldville, declared June 12 that Adoula had been unwilling to make concessions on this point. He charged that Adoula was negotiating "with the conviction that if the talks fail the United Nations will pass a resolution to integrate Katanga by force." Tshombe walked out of the conference June 20-21, charging that central government troops again had attacked in the Kongolo and Baudouinville areas of northern Katanga. The meetings resumed again June 22, after a joint UN-Katanga commission had found no evidence of renewed fighting in Katanga, but were broken off finally June 26.

Tshombe returned to Elisabethville June 26. He blamed Adoula for the break in the talks but said he would be willing to resume the negotiations in the near future. Adoula asserted, however, that Tshombe had rejected any agreement "no matter what terms were discussed." He added: "We made our effort. Now it is up to the United Nations to take the responsibility of restoring our unity." Acting Secy. Gen. Thant reported to his Congo advisory committee June 29 that the question that remained was the decisive one as to whether the Katanga regime would persist in its secession.

Women Attack UN Troops

2,000 Katangan troops paraded without incident July 11 in Elisabethville ceremonies marking the Katanga regime's 2d anniversary of secession. UN officials protested that the parade violated an agreement to limit the number of marchers to 300 to avoid possible provocation. The UN Force retaliated by setting up a road block on the route used by the parade, the only major road from the center of Elisabethville that had not been subject to control by UN troops.

Indian troops manning the Elisabethville roadblock were attacked July 17 by mobs of African women. The women, estimated to number 10,000, were members of the Association of Katangan Women, a militant organization formed by leaders of the Tshombe regime. The mobs fought the Indians for more than 3 hours with clubs, stones and fists before they were dispersed by baton charges and shots fired in the air. Katangan authorities said that one woman and 2 children had been killed by the Indians' shots. Gardiner, protesting the attack July 18, said that one woman and a child had been killed—but by Katanga gendarmes who had attempted to make it appear that their shots came from the embattled UN troops. Gardiner told Tshombe that the women's march was "premeditated and organized for political ends" by Katanga authorities.

Adoula Revises Cabinet

A major revision of the central Congolese cabinet was carried out by Premier Adoula July 11. More than ½ of the cabinet's 43 members, among them the reputed leaders of the leftist and rightist factions, were dismissed. Foreign Min. Justin Bomboko, Interior Min. Cleophas Kamitatu and Vice Premier Jason Sendwe were retained, but Joseph Ileo, information minister and former premier, and Vice Premiers Jean Bolikango and Christophe Gbenye were among those dropped. The new cabinet was approved July 16 by a 60-44 vote of the Congolese Parliament. 17 deputies were absent and 6 abstained from voting on the cabinet.

Adoula, replying in Parliament in June 14 to charges that his government was corrupt and incompetent, had declared: "Every one of you wanted to become a minister. To satisfy these ambitions we have been forced to constitute a government of dishonest and incapable persons chosen by you."

(A 2-day general strike called by the Union of Congolese Workers to protest government ministers' high salaries—$2,000 monthly, plus $900 for expenses, compared with $1.50 per day for the average Congolese urban worker—had been put down by troops Apr. 2. All public meetings were banned and hundreds of unionists were arrested, among them Pres. Andre Bo-Boliko of the UCW. Bo-Boliko was tried on subversion charges but was acquitted Apr. 10.)

New Constitution Drafted

A draft program for the writing of a new Congolese constitution that would assure Katanga and other provinces a wide range of self-government was outlined by Adoula July 29. The Adoula proposal, offered as a basis for new negotiations on unifying the Congo, would grant the provinces responsibility for local administration, economic affairs and the maintenance of public order within their borders. The central government was to be transformed into a federal institution responsible for foreign affairs, defense, monetary affairs, trade, customs and communications. Adoula, in a personal message to U Thant, asked UN jurists to aid in drawing up the constitution. The Adoula program was welcomed enthusiastically by Tshombe July 30, and Thant sent the requested UN constitutional experts to the Congo.

A proposed federal constitution largely embodying these principles was submitted by Adoula to the Chamber of Deputies Oct. 16. 2 key features, considered major concessions to Tshombe, would: (a) guarantee each province 50% of royalties on minerals mined in its territory and give each province the right to grant mineral concessions; (b) guarantee each province the right to elect its own legislature and governor, to levy local taxes, command its own police and establish its schools.

PRESSURE GROWS FOR SETTLEMENT

UN Plans Economic Sanctions

A renewal of violence in Katanga, coupled with the breakdown of the Tshombe-Adoula negotiations and the continued threat of a new round in the Congolese civil war, gave rise to new pressure for a settlement in the Congo.

A new UN proposal for unifying the Congo developed from appeals by Acting Secy. Gen. Thant in July for economic measures against the Katanga regime. His program for economic action was taken up with his Congo advisory committee in New York July 24 on his return from a European tour during which he had sounded out several nations on the subject. Thant discussed his proposals with interested nations during the following weeks, modified them as result of these discussions, and finally presented them to the Security Council Aug. 20 in a report on UN operations in the Congo. (Speaking at a Helsinki press conference July 20, during his European tour, Thant had said: "Mr. Tshombe is a very unstable man. . . . The same can be said of his 2 colleagues, Mr. Munongo, who pretends to be the interior minister of Katanga, and Mr. Kimbe, who pretends to be the foreign minister. I have tried to get Tshombe and the central government to negotiate, but without any results. I don't know what I can do with such a bunch of clowns.")

Thant's report outlined these proposals for creating Congolese national unity: (1) Completion of the new Congolese constitution; (2) reconstitution of the central Congolese government to "provide representation for all political and provincial groups"; (3) laws "to establish definitive arrangements for the division of revenues between the central and provincial governments"; (4) a temporary agreement by Katanga and the central government "to share on a 50-50 basis revenues from all taxes or duties . . . and all royalties from mining concessions," with assurances that 50% of the foreign exchange earned by Katanga would be returned to the province for its essential needs; (5) formation of a UN-Congo-Katanga committee to prepare within 30 days a plan for "unification of the entire Congolese army" within 2 months.

Thant warned that if Katanga failed to accept the program, he would call on member states to impose a total embargo on the province and particularly on its major mineral exports, copper and cobalt. An appeal for worldwide support of the proposal had been made by Thant July 31-Aug. 1 in messages to all 104 UN member states. Thant's messages, made public Aug. 1, called on UN members to use their influence to restore the Congo's unity; it asked them to consider economic sanctions if the Tshombe regime refused to end its secession. Thant confirmed Aug. 2 that he had urged the Union Miniere du Haut-Katanga to withhold tax and royalty payments to the Katanga government until agreement had been reached on reunifying the Congo. He said at a UN news conference that the UN Force was prepared to protect the mining firm's installations and equipment against reprisals by Katanga if it complied. (Managing director Richard Terwagne of Union Miniere declared Aug. 9 that his firm had no choice but to continue its payments to Katanga authorities. He said: Union Miniere facilities were scattered over 6,000 square miles where "the Katangese gendarmerie is in complete control"; it would be impossible to give UN protection against "saboteurs or other hostile forces"; Katanga officials had made clear that they would use force to compel the firm to continue its payments. These payments to Katanga were estimated to have totaled $40 million in 1961.)

Support Given Sanctions Plan

The Western powers—particularly the U.S., Britain and Belgium—had resumed talks on the Congo in mid-July. Although all 3 agreed on the necessity of supporting UN measures to force new political negotiations between Katanga and the central government, Britain made it clear that it would not take part in economic sanctions against

Katanga. A Western working paper embodying the principal views and suggestions of the U.S., Britain and Belgium was approved at a Washington meeting of representatives of the 3 governments Aug. 2 and was submitted to Thant Aug. 3. The document, which did not have the formal approval of the 3 governments, proposed that the Congo be offered massive aid on the attainment of political and economic unity. The paper suggested that aid and political pressures be used to induce Katanga to end its secession but that further Katangan resistance be met with economic sanctions.

A U.S. plan for ending Katanga's secession was presented to the UN Aug. 9 after the British government reportedly had informed Washington that it would not support the sanctions envisaged in the Western working paper. The U.S. plan was not made public, but it was said to parallel closely the Western paper in offering aid and other inducements for Katanga's acquiescence and in calling for a strict economic boycott of the province if it refused. The U.S. program was offered as a replacement for the joint Western plan, reportedly on the ground that it would permit Britain and Belgium to cooperate in persuading Katanga to abandon its secession but would not bind them to join in sanctions.

Thant's July 24 plan for economic sanctions if necessary to restore Congolese unity was assured the support of the U.S., Britain, Belgium and the central Congolese govern in a series of government statements issued Aug. 24-26. Soviet press and radio reaction was critical of the plan, and a rival Russian proposal transmitted to the UN Sept. 6 called for UN action to end Katanga's secession and extend the central government's control to the province within one month, after which all UN forces would be withdrawn from the Congo. The Soviet note dismissed the UN plan as an attempt to weaken the central Congolese government and to prevent reunification.

The UN proposals were presented to Katanga Foreign Min. Evariste Kimba in Elisabethville Aug. 24 by UN Undersecy. Gardiner. Gardiner gave the Katanga regime 10 days to accept or reject the UN plan and begin talks on its implementation.

Katanga Accepts Reunification

Tshombe announced Katanga's acceptance of the UN plan "with enthusiasm" Sept. 3 in notes to UN authorities and the U.S., British and Belgian consuls in Elisabethville. The notes proposed that special commissions be created to work out procedures for unifying Katangan and Congolese armed forces and dividing Katanga's revenues from mining operations. But Tshombe declared in speeches in Elisabethville Sept. 12-14 that the UN plan was a ruse for the overthrow of the Katanga government and that no peaceful settlement was possible unless the UN and central government halted attacks on the province.

UN proposals for immediate action to carry out the plan were presented to the Katanga and central Congolese governments Sept. 11. They were accepted by Premier Adoula the same day, and Tshombe informed UN authorities Sept. 17 of his willingness to open talks on the plan despite recurring UN-Katanga fighting and what he charged were plans by Maj. Gen. Joseph D. Mobutu, Congolese army commander, for a "general attack" on Katanga.

Further Katanga Fighting Reported

An outbreak of fighting between Katanga troops and forces of the central government was reported Aug. 16 near Kyayo, south of Albertville. A central government communique asserted that Katanga soldiers had fired on Congolese troops and were advancing toward Albertville, in northern Katanga, burning villages in their path. UN Undersecy. Gardiner announced Aug. 17 that he had warned Kimba the UN would intervene "with all the means at its disposal" unless the Katangan attacks were halted. Further Katangan attacks, on central government troops, this time along the Kabongo-Kabalo railway, were reported by the UN Aug. 19.

Tshombe charged Sept. 12 that 2 Katangan gendarmes had been killed earlier that day when their unit was attacked on the Elisabethville-Kipushi highway by a superior force of Indian UN troops. He asserted Sept. 13 that UN planes had dropped incendiary bombs on an outlying district of Elisabethville and that UN aircraft had flown 2,000 central government troops to Kabalo, in northern Katanga, in preparation for a general offensive against his regime. UN authorities conceded that fighting had occurred on the Elisabethville-Kipushi highway, but they said Katangan gendarmes had staged the incident and that no one had been killed. They denied that UN planes had attacked Elisabethville or had flown Congolese troops to northern Katanga.

Following Tshombe's Sept. 17 charge that the central government was readying a "general attack," Gardiner promised Sept. 18 that UN planes would patrol northern Katanga. UN authorities in Leopoldville reported Sept. 19 that preliminary aerial reconnaissance had disclosed "no significant troop movements or military concentrations" such as would be needed for an offensive against Katanga. The UN said there was no basis for Katangan charges, made in a military communique issued the same day in Elisabethville, that 1,000 Congolese troops and Baluba tribesmen were attacking Pweto, 200 miles north of the capital, and that 2,000 to 3,000 Congolese troops were entering Katanga from South Kasai Province. Gardiner charged in a Sept. 25 letter to Tshombe that Katanga was continuing to recruit mercenaries abroad for its military forces. He said soldiers were being hired through newspaper ads. Gardiner reported to Thant Oct. 9 that Katanga's mercenary forces had been increased to their former peak strength of 300-500 men and that its air force was in the midst of a major buildup.

A truce in north Katanga (which Premier Adoula said was a separate province and not part of Tshombe-ruled Katanga) was signed in Elisabethville Oct. 16 by representatives of the central government, Katanga and the UN. It provided for an exchange of prisoners and the cessation of all police and troop movements in the area. But north Katanga fighting broke out again within 4 days. Katanga Foreign Min. Kimba charged Oct. 20 that Katangan forces had been attacked on the pretext they had shot down a UN reconnaissance plane Oct. 14 and had bombed villages and central government troop positions. Kimba said the plane's loss was used by Gardiner as "a justification . . . for the aggressive action against Katanga."

The UN command in Leopoldville Nov. 12 ordered UN fighter planes to attack if Katangan aircraft continued offensive operations. The decision was made after the UN had made public "fairly reliable" reports that about 70 bombs had been dropped in north Katanga by Katangan bombers. The Katangan government Nov. 12 formally denied the reports. It asserted that the bombing charge had been made to justify military action against Katanga.

The central government reported Dec. 5 that its troops had captured Kongolo, which had been defended by some 1,500 Katangan troops.

Economic Reprisals Threatened

Gardiner delivered to Tshombe Dec. 10 a "final warning" from U Thant that the UN would ask UN member nations to boycott the exports of Katanga's copper and cobalt mines if Tshombe did not take immediate steps to end Katanga's secession. Letters from Thant asking for an immediate boycott of Katanga copper and cobalt were sent to Britain, Belgium, Portugal and South Africa Dec. 13. Thant sent similar letters Dec. 14 to Austria, Brazil, Denmark, France, India, Italy, Japan, the Netherlands, Sweden, Switzerland, the U.S. and West Germany. The central Congolese government Dec. 12 had asked the same 16 countries and Southern Rhodesia to stop buying copper and cobalt from Katanga. The Congolese said its request was made under Thant's plan for use of economic pressure to reunify the Congo.

Belgian Foreign Min. Paul-Henri Spaak had conferred with Thant and U.S. officials at UN headquarters in New York Nov. 26 and with Pres. Kennedy at the White House Nov. 27. Spaak and Mr. Kennedy issued a joint communique warning Katanga that sanctions might be invoked unless early action were taken on reunifying the Congo. Gardiner told the UN Security Council Nov. 29 that Katanga would be subject to increasing economic pressures— and military force, if necessary—if Tshombe did not act soon on Thant's proposals.

A partial blockade of Katanga had been attempted early in August but apparently had been ineffective. The UN Command had announced in Elisabethville Aug. 6 that all unauthorized air traffic over Katanga had been banned on orders of the central government. A communique issued in Leopoldville Aug. 7 by the central government had ordered the "total suspension" of all Katanga radio broadcasts and telecommunications with outside areas. The central government ordered foreign businesses to choose between operations in Katanga and the rest of the Congo. But except for the controls on air traffic, no effort was reported to have been made to enforce the central government orders.

U.S. Studies Arms Aid for UN

A U.S. military mission headed by Lt. Gen. Louis W. Truman made an on-the-spot survey of Katanga and other parts of the Congo Dec. 21-26, on Pres. Kennedy's orders, to determine the types of U.S. military equipment that "might be useful" to the UN forces there and to check on whether UN troops could maintain order in event of increased Soviet pressure or if the UN used strong measures in Katanga. About 100-150 Katanga University students stoned the U.S. consulate in Elisabethville Dec. 20 in protest against reported U.S. plans to send more military aid to the UN forces.

(Controversy arose in the U.S. over efforts to deport Michel Struelens, Belgian director of Katanga Information Services in the U.S. and Tshombe's "official representative" in New York. Struelens had been an alien without legal status in the U.S. since Sept. 1961, when the U.S. Immigration and Naturalization Service had invalidated his Belgian passport and his permit to work as a journalist in the U.S. The State Department Dec. 4 opposed his request for a change of his status to that of an alien admitted for permanent residence, and the Immigration Service ordered him Dec. 6 to leave the country voluntarily within 15 days or face deportation. After a new hearing Dec. 17, the Immigration Service ruled again Dec. 26 that Struelens must quit the country. By the year's end, however, Struelens was still in the U.S. fighting deportation and was receiving increasing support for his cause from Congress members, notably members of the Senate Internal Security Subcommittee.)

Other Secessionists Remain Active

Albert Kalonji, self-proclaimed king of the Baluba tribes and of South Kasai Province, won his freedom from a prison near Leopoldville Sept. 8 and was flown to Bakwanga, capital of South Kasai. Congolese police officials, disclosing his departure, charged Sept. 9 that he had escaped with the connivance of government authorities. But Leopoldville Province officials replied that he had been released on the authority of the provincial interior minister. Kalonji had been convicted and sentenced to 5 years in prison by a Leopoldville court Apr. 20 on charges of illegal arrest and torture of political opponents. During his imprisonment, the virtually independent South Kasai regime had been run by Ferdinand Kazadi.

In a broadcast from Bakwanga Sept. 9, Kalonji "thanked" the central government for arranging his release and pledged to support its efforts to create a unified and federal Congo. But the central government was forced to proclaim a state of emergency in South Kasai Sept. 30 to counter what it said was a new "pro-Kalonjist" uprising by elements of the dissident province's 3,000-man military force. The UN Command said Oct. 2 that its Kasai representative, Eric Packham, had reported that central government troops and gendarmes had put down the uprising and had placed Kalonji and his ministers under house arrest. Kalonji escaped early in October and arrived Oct. 12 in Elisabethville, the Katanga capital. Gen. Floribert Dinanga, who had commanded Kalonji's gendarmerie, was captured by central government troops Oct. 13.

Anicet Kashamura, information minister in the late Patrice Lumumba's cabinet, said in Rabat, Morocco, Sept. 28 that 4 leftwing groups had united to form the National Congolese Movement of Resistance. Kashamura said its immediate goal was the ouster of the Adoula regime. The 4 parties : National Congolese Movement (Lumumba followers); African Solidarity Party (headed by the imprisoned Antoine Gizenga); Center of African Regroupment (headed by Kashamura); Balubakat tribal group (headed by Jason Sendwe).

The Congolese Chamber of Deputies Nov. 23 approved a resolution giving the Adoula regime 24 hours to release Christophe Gbenye and 3 other opposition deputies arrested in October for an alleged secessionist plot. The 4 deputies were freed Nov. 26, and a special commission reported to Parliament Dec. 7 that the charges against them were false. The chamber Dec. 7 then rejected Justice Min. Chretien Weregemere's request that it lift Gbenye's parliamentary immunity, and it voted by 76-4 to censure Weregemere for his role in the arrest of the deputies.

THIRD UN ASSAULT ON KATANGA

Solution by Force Sought

Troops of the UN Force attacked objectives in Elisabethville and other parts of Katanga Province Dec. 29 in what appeared to be a major attempt to end Katanga's secession. The UN attack, begun by infantry supported by aerial strafing and bombardment, was said to have been launched in response to prior attacks by Katanga forces. But this version was disputed by many observers in Katanga. The attack was the 3d major UN military offensive against the Katanga regime. 2 assaults in April and December 1961 had ended indecisively.

UN units commanded by Indian Brig. Reginald Noronha seized almost complete control of Elisabethville in their initial thrust Dec. 29 and were reported advancing on the military stronghold of Kolwezi—a mining town about 150 miles northwest of Elisabethville—by Dec. 31. Kamina (260 miles northwest of Elisabethville) and Kipushi (about 15 miles from Elisabethville on the Northern Rhodesian border) fell Dec. 30 to UN contingents from Ghana and Ireland. Gen. Prem Chand, Indian commander of the UN forces in Katanga, said Dec. 30 that his casualties were 2 Indians and 2 Ethiopians killed and 14 Ethiopians, 10 Indians, an Irishman and a Tunisian wounded. The bodies of 50 Africans—reportedly killed in 4 days of fighting between Katangans and UN troops—were found in Elisabethville's outskirts.

U Thant called on Tshombe Dec. 31 to negotiate with the central government on Katanga's reentry into the Congo within 2 weeks or face "other measures." Thant gave this account of the start of the UN offensive: Katangan troops had fired intermittently "and at times heavily" Dec. 22-28 on UN roadblocks in the Elisabethville area; early Dec. 28 "Tshombe sought to stop his troops from firing, but . . . he did not succeed in doing so; later in the day, although he again agreed to bring about a cessation of firing and also agreed that the gendarmerie roadblocks and strong points from which the fire was coming should be removed, he refused to sign a statement to this effect; consequently, since the firing persisted, in midafternoon of the 28th, the United Nations troops, in self-defense, were ordered at last to protect their security and their freedom of movement by clearing away the roadblocks and strong points." Thant said that "the United Nations is seeking no victory and no surrender in Katanga, for the United Nations is not waging war against anyone in that province." He added, however, that the UN supported the central government "as the only legitimate government of the Congo."

Dispute Over Attack

The UN offensive against Katanga was supported by the U.S. but was opposed by Britain, Belgium and France. A British Foreign Office statement noted Dec. 29 that "the British government has repeatedly impressed upon U Thant the futility of trying to impose a political settlement on the Congo by force." About 250 persons demonstrated outside the U.S. embassy in Brussels Dec. 29 in protest against U.S. support of UN operations in Katanga. Belgium called on the UN Dec. 30 to halt military operations in the Congo.

Tshombe, who reportedly had flown to Salisbury, Southern Rhodesia Dec. 30 in a Rhodesia air force plane, said Dec. 30 that the UN had started the current fighting and that the U.S. must take full blame for it.

Sen. Thomas J. Dodd (D., Conn.) Dec. 31 called the UN offensive in Katanga a "flagrant, inhuman act of aggression." He said the matter should be investigated by a private, international legal group . Sen. Barry Goldwater (R., Ariz.) said Dec. 31: "The bitterness generated by the unjust UN war against Moise Tshombe, the only full-fledged pro-Western leader in the Congo, will last for a long time and make effective unification of the area a total impossibility."

1963

UN military forces won a total victory over the troops of the separatist Katanga Province regime, occupying all major Katangan industrial and population centers. Katangan Pres. Moise Tshombe acknowledged the defeat and pledged an end to Katangan secessionism; he then left the Congo to go into exile in Europe. The central government extended its administrative control to the province, site of the Congo's huge mining resources, but promised not to take retaliation on Katangans who had supported the Tshombe regime. Katangan representatives later were given prominent posts in a new 'government of national reconciliation' formed by Premier Adoula.

KATANGA REGIME SURRENDERS

UN Troops Crush Dissidence

The 2½-year campaign to prevent Katanga Province's secession from the Congo was ended successfully in January after UN Force troops occupied Katanga's cities and military and mining centers. Katanga Pres. Moise-Kapenda Tshombe, acknowledging the defeat of his government's gendarmerie, submitted to the control of Premier Cyrille Adoula's central Congolese government in Leopoldville and agreed to end his fight for the independence of the mineral-rich province.

Events leading to the UN's victory over the Katanga regime:

Indian troops of the UN force moved southward through Katanga Jan. 1 and crossed the Lufira River, 20 miles from Jadotville, one of the principal centers of Katangan resistance. The Indian units were said to have encountered little resistance. The Lufira crossing was made difficult by the destruction of bridges by retreating Katangan gendarmes, led by white mercenary officers, but the Indians forded the river and brought their vehicles across on make-shift rafts. (UN Secy. Gen. U Thant had assured British and Belgium envoys at the UN that the UN troops would halt at the Lufira. They did not stop there, and it was charged later that Thant had permitted the offensive to continue when it became clear that a final Katangan defeat was imminent.)

Pres. Tshombe called Jan. 1 for a cease-fire and for negotiations on terms for ending his government's secession. Tshombe's appeal was made in a message relayed to UN officials from his temporary headquarters in Jadotville. In a 2d message from Jadotville, received in Leopoldville Jan. 2, Tshombe appealed for an immediate meeting with a UN representative to discuss ending the fighting. In the Jan. 2 message, Tshombe affirmed "my adherence to the U Thant plan," a proposal advanced by Secy. Gen. Thant in August 1962 for reunifying the Congo on the basis of a federal constitution.

The Tshombe appeals were rejected by Thant Jan. 2. Spokesmen at UN headquarters in New York asserted that Thant wanted "actions by Mr. Tshombe and not words, written or oral." They said: Thant felt that "it is now too late for negotiations"; he expected Tshombe to acquiesce in the UN's total occupation of Katanga and in the assumption of his regime's national functions—foreign affairs, customs, defense—by representatives of the central Congolese government.

Jadotville was captured without fighting Jan. 3 by UN troops commanded by Indian Brig. Reginald S. Noronha. UN forces, which had taken Elisabethville, Katanga's capital, and had seized nearby Kipushi (on the Rhodesian border) as well as Kamina, thus controlled all major communications points with the exception of Kolwezi and its airbase. (The capital and other strongholds had fallen to the UN in the first 3 days of its offensive, Dec. 29-31, 1962.) Tshombe, who had fled to Kolwezi before the UN forces reached Jadotville, told AP reporter Adrian Porter Jan. 4 that he would continue the fight even if Kolwezi fell.

The U.S. called on Tshombe Jan. 4 to acquiesce in the UN's demands for the integration of Katanga with the rest of the Congo. It did so in a statement that made clear U.S. support of the UN's military action. The statement asserted that the UN forces in Katanga "now occupy most key populated areas and mining centers." It urged Tshombe to "end promptly the Katanga secession by recognizing the UN's full freedom of movement throughout Katanga . . . and by exerting his influence with Katangese military personnel and the civilian population to prevent sabotage and damage to important installations." "Mr. Tshombe should also make himself available immediately to cooperate with the UN . . . and to put into effect other practical arrangements to carry out swiftly the clear provisions of the U Thant plan," the statement said.

The UN ultimatum and U.S. statement brought no immediate response from Tshombe despite the apparent collapse of Katangan resistance and the steady advance of UN forces into all corners of the province.

Tshombe Detained by UN

Tshombe returned to Elisabethville and was put under house arrest Jan. 9 on Thant's orders. He had flown from Kolwezi to Kipushi and then had driven with the Belgian consul to Elisabethville.

In a٦ interview granted on his arrival in Elisabethville Jan. 8 Tshombe defied the UN and Adoula to try to integrate Katanga in the Congo against its wishes. He said: "My ministers and I have been very busy in Kolwezi planning the demolition of all industries. In that case Adoula, the UN or we will have lost everything." (Union Miniere said in statements issued at UN headquarters in New York and in Brussels Jan. 8 that Katanga police had mined dams and power stations and had occupied all of its pits and plants in the Kolwezi area. But, despite reports that Katangan troops had carried out extensive sabotage of the Jadotville facilities of Union Miniere, the damage was found to be confined to the nearby Shituru cobalt refinery. Union Miniere announced Jan. 6, however, that it had been forced to suspend all production in Katanga.)

UN authorities freed Tshombe Jan. 10 after he agreed to help reestablish order in Katanga by persuading his troops to lay down their arms.

Katanga Surrenders

The secessionist regime's surrender to the UN and the authority of the central government was announced by Tshombe Jan. 15 in Kolwezi, his government's last stronghold. Reading to newsmen from messages addressed to U Thant and Adoula, Tshombe declared: "I am ready to proclaim immediately before the world that Katanga's secession is ended, to grant the United Nations troops liberty of movement throughout Katanga, and to return to Elisabethville to direct the means of applying the U Thant plan." In his letter to Adoula, Tshombe urged that the central Congolese government stand by its pledges of amnesty for himself, members of his cabinet and all others who had served his regime. He asserted that his decision to surrender had been made to spare Katanga fighting that would end in "a total military victory" for the UN and would "plunge the Congolese people into misery to the profit of foreign interests."

A formal Katanga surrender agreement was signed in Elisabethville Jan. 17 by Tshombe, Gen. Prem Chand, UN Force commander in Katanga, and George Sherry, the acting UN civil representative in the province.

Terms of the surrender: (1) Tshombe was to insure that the UN's occupation of Kolwezi "shall take place peacefully, with the cooperation of all concerned, including the gendarmerie and local authorities"; (2) the UN was to enter Kolwezi by Jan. 21; (3) UN troops would assure the safety of Katangan gendarmes pending their integration into the regular Congolese armed forces; (4) gendarmerie units were to surrender their arms and ammunition to a special UN detachment; (5) Katangan authorities were to cooperate in the removal of explosives placed to sabotage Kolwezi installations.

Tshombe returned to Kolwezi Jan. 19 to persuade his troops to lay down their arms and not to set off the explosives they had set in mining facilities and public buildings. UN troops occupied Kolwezi peacefully Jan. 21, putting an end to all armed Katangan resistance. In an emotional address to 2,000 armed Katangan gendarmes Jan. 21, an hour before the UN occupation, Tshombe pleaded with his men to accept their defeat and work for a new Katanga. The UN troops were led into Kolwezi by Brig. Noronha and a truce delegation made up of Katangan officials, gendarmerie officers and officials of Union Miniere.

Central Government Takes Control

Premier Adoula moved quickly to impose central government authority in Katanga. Ex-Premier Joseph Ileo, Leopoldville's resident minister in Katanga, arrived in Elisabethville Jan. 23 to take charge of measures for the reintegration of the province with the Congo. Gen. Joseph Mobutu, commander-in-chief of the Congolese army, arrived in Elisabethville Jan. 24 to supervise the integration of the Katanga gendarmerie in the central forces.

Ileo, in a radio speech to the Katangan people Jan. 25, assured them that he had come to Katanga to arrange "national reconciliation and nothing else." He pledged to respect "the prerogative of the provincial authority and the assembly which elected them." Ileo met with Tshombe and the Katanga cabinet Jan. 29 to discuss integration details. Gen. Norbert Muke, commander of the Katanga gendarmerie, flew to Leopoldville Feb. 6 to swear allegiance to the central government.

In a report delivered to the Security Council on the developments in Katanga, Secy. Gen. Thant declared Jan. 29 that he had "reasonable confidence that the phase of active military involvement by United Nations forces in the Congo is about over." He said that with the successful termination of the military action in Katanga, the UN planned to reduce its Congo force from its current strength of 19,000 troops and technicians to 12,000-13,000 by Mar. 30. He said that a reduced UN Congo force would be required for an extended period to maintain order and help the Congolese government cope with tribal unrest. In a further report prepared for the Security Council and made public Feb. 6, Thant warned that despite the UN's apparent victory a "too rapid withdrawal" of troops from Katanga could encourage the revival of secessionism. (The 5,626-man Indian contingent of the UN Force began withdrawing from the Congo Mar. 16.)

'Reconciliation' Government Formed

A "government of national reconciliation" was formed by Premier Adoula Apr. 17. The new government included members of every Congolese political party with the exception of extremists pledged to oust the Adoula regime. A number of former ministers were ousted or demoted. Among these was Foreign Min. Justin M. Bomboko, named justice minister, a less important post. Auguste Kalanda-Mabika, 30, a lecturer at the National School of Administration and Law, was named foreign minister. The National Congolese Movement, the late Patrice Lumumba's party, gained 3 new ministries and became the strongest single party in the cabinet.

Representatives of Katanga, which had not been represented in the previous cabinet, were named to 4 important posts. The 4 Katangan ministers: Jacques Masangu, a vice prime minister: Bertin Mwanba, a deputy foreign minister; Albert Nyembo, national economy minister; Rodolphe Yava, foreign trade minister.

The new cabinet: Prime Minister—Adoula; Vice Prime Minister for Economic Coordination—Joseph Kasongo; Vice Prime Minister for Social Questions—Masangu; Foreign Affairs—Kalanda-Mabika; Defense—Jerome Anany; Interior —Joseph Maboti; Justice—Bomboko; Information and Tourism—Antoine-Roger Bolamba; Planning and Industrial Development—Cleophas Kamitatu; National Economy—Nyembo; Finance—Emmanuel Bamba; Middle Classes and Community Development—Joseph Lutula; Lands, Mines and Power— Alexandre Mahamba; Transportation and Communications— Alphonse Ilunga; Posts and Telegraph—Ferdinand Mungamba; Agriculture—Constant Tshela-Muana; Foreign Trade— Yava; Public Works—Albert Delvaux; National Education— Michel Colin; Public Health—Paul Bolya; Labor—Alphonse Nguvulu; Public Affairs—Alois Kabangi; Social Affairs— Jacques Massa; Youth and Sports—Honore Agoyo; State Min. for Katangan Affairs—Joseph Ileo; Deputy, Foreign Affairs—Mwamba; State Secretaries—Marcel Lengema (Foreign Affairs), Nestor Watum (Defense), Celestin Lunyasi (Interior), Paul Katanga (Information and Tourism), Justin Matiti (National Education), Antoine Ngwenza (Public Works), Honore Mukengele (National Economy), Michel Denge (Agriculture), Francois Kupa (Finance).

The Congolese Chamber of Deputies voted May 21 and the Senate voted May 28 to create a new province of Lualaba in the western region of South Katanga. The area was the homeland of the Lunda tribe, whose political support had been a mainstay of the Tshombe regime. Kolwezi became part of the new province. The Senate June 25 completed passage of a bill to incorporate the rest of South Katanga into the new province of East Katanga. Pres. Joseph Kasavubu signed both bills into law July 9. Edouard Bulundwe, a member of Tshombe's Conakat party, was elected president of East Katanga Aug. 13.

Tshombe Flees to Europe

A combined force of UN and central government troops disarmed Tshombe's personal guard in a pre-dawn raid on the presidential palace in Elisabethville May 24. The UN command, which originally had consented to Tshombe's retention of an armed personal guard, now contended that it was a violation of the agreement for the integration of the Katanga gendarmerie with the Congolese army.

Tshombe disappeared from Elisabethville May 29, after the central government had announced its discovery of a new plot to renew Katanga's dissidence. Tshombe's supporters claimed that the announcement clearly had been intended to serve as justification for Tshombe's arrest. Tshombe left the Congo via Southern Rhodesia and flew June 6 to Paris, ostensibly for medical treatment for eye and stomach disorders. Tshombe remained in Europe for the duration of 1963. He said he intended to return to the Congo and work loyally with the central government. But he was reported several times to have conferred with mercenary leaders and businessmen linked with the former Katanga secessionist movement and these meetings gave rise to widespread reports that he planned a new attempt to wrest Katanga from control of the Leopoldville government.

Belgian Aid, Soviet Ousters

Belgium agreed Aug. 31 to provide the Congo with more than $1 billion in investment aid and technical assistance. The agreement was signed in Leopoldville Aug. 31 by Count Charles de Kerchove de Denterghem, Belgian ambassador to the Congo, and Marcel Lengema, Congolese State Secretary for Foreign Affairs. A preliminary agreement had been reached in Brussels Aug. 2 by delegations headed by Premier Adoula and Belgian Foreign Min. Paul-Henri Spaak. (It was disclosed July 20 that the U.S. had suspended its import and public works grants to the Congo in an effort to force the Congo to devalue its franc and make other fiscal and economic reforms. The 2 categories accounted for about half of the U.S.' Congolese aid program, totaling about $73 million in the year ended June 30.)

The Congolese government expelled the entire 100-member Soviet embassy staff Nov. 21 in the aftermath of the arrest of 2 embassy members on charges of attempting to undermine the Adoula government. The 2 Russians—embassy counselor Boris S. Voronin and embassy press attache Yuri N. Myakotnykh—had been beaten and arrested Nov. 19 as they returned to Leopoldville by ferry from the neighboring city of Brazzaville. They allegedly carried documents linking them with a plot to overthrow the Adoula regime. A 3d Soviet diplomat and 2 Czechs were also arrested late Nov. 19 by Congolese paratroops who surrounded the Soviet embassy. Voronin and Myakotnykh were released Nov. 21 and ordered to leave the country within 48 hours. Adoula said Nov. 21 that papers found on the 2 Russians indicated that they were working with a National Liberation Committee that had been formed in Brazzaville by Christophe Gbenye, a supporter of the late Patrice Lumumba.

1964

Followers of the late Patrice Lumumba revived their rebel movement in 1964 and, with Communist military and political support, began an offensive that won them control of the northern and eastern parts of the Congo. Despite the renewal of fighting, the Congolese government made no effort to obtain extension of the UN Force's mandate, and UN troops were withdrawn from the country at mid-year. Responding to threats against Europeans and Americans held hostage in rebel territory, the U.S. and Belgium, acting with Leopoldville's assent, dropped paratroops on Stanleyville and other rebel centers and saved most of the imprisoned whites. The successful U.S.-Belgian operation was used as an opening wedge in a new central government attempt to destroy the rebel movement.

COMMUNIST-BACKED REVOLTS SPREAD

Gizenga Followers Win Kwilu, Kivu

Communist-supported revolts spread through the Congo's northern and eastern provinces early in 1964 and continued through most of the year.

Pres. Joseph Kasavubu Jan. 21 declared a state of emergency in western Kwilu Province, where rebellious tribesmen had seized control of 1/3 of the territory. The rebellion was reported Jan. 25 to have spread to neigboring Kasai and Kwango Provinces. The rebels were led by former Education Min. Pierre Mulele, 34, a Peiping-oriented leftist. He had served as ambassador to the UAR for the deposed secessionist Stanleyville regime that had been headed by Antoine Gizenga, currently in prison. Mulele, secretary general of Gizenga's leftist African Solidarity Party, had returned to the Congo in the summer of 1963 after 18 months of exile in Cairo and Communist China.

2 companies of Congolese gendarmes mutinied at Stanleyville's Keteke military camp Jan. 28, and about 300 followers of the late leftist Premier Patrice Lumumba simultaneously staged anti-government demonstrations in Stanleyville. Participants in both actions demanded the release from prison of former Eastern Province Gov. Georges Grenfell, a leader of the province's Lumumbist Congolese National Movement. The mutineers were finally disarmed Jan. 29 and order was restored in Stanleyville.

The central government started to airlift troop reinforcements to Kwilu Province Jan. 31, and the UN flew supplies and rations to rebel-infested areas. The main fighting centered around Idiofa, where a 40-man government garrison was under repeated rebel attack. Lt. Col. Eugene Abeya, 45, Congolese army chief of staff, was killed Feb. 6 while leading reinforcements to the besieged Kwilu garrison of Gungu, where guerrillas Feb. 21 killed 32 civilian residents.

The rebels had won control of most of eastern Kwilu Province by early spring.

Leftwing terrorists captured Uvira in Kivu Province May 15 without firing a shot and set up another rebel administration. Premier Cyrille Adoula appealed May 31 for UN troops to quell the revolt in Kivu. Congolese government troops were reported fleeing Bukavu, the provincial capital, after being routed by rebels.

A rebel force June 19 captured the North Katanga capital of Albertville and routed the 900-man military garrison. The rebels were reported June 22 to have formed a revolutionary government headed by followers of Mulele. Albertville had been captured May 27 by the Jeunesse—a rebel youth group—armed with bows and arrows. In retaking the city May 29, Congolese troops had killed 100 civilians.

U.S. Pilots Fly Against Rebels

Kivu rebel Col. Louis Bidalira charged June 11 that U.S. T–28 fighter planes had bombed insurgent strongholds earlier that day near Kamaniola in the Ruzizi Valley. Bidalira denounced the attack as a "cruel and savage intervention against defenseless Congolese." (Kamaniola, held by the rebels for 2 weeks, was recaptured by government troops following rocket attacks made by allegedly U.S.-piloted T-28s. 50 rebels were slain in the fighting.)

The State Department, acknowledging June 15 that the U.S. had given the Congo several T-28 planes, denied reports that Americans were flying them under private contract with the Leopoldville government. But the department conceded the following day that "some American pilots under contract with the Congolese government have flown T-28 sorties in the last few days in the eastern part of the Congo." It announced June 17 that U.S. civilian pilots no longer would fly combat missions in the Congo. The announcement said: "The contractual arrangements between the American technicians and the Congolese government do not violate any law of the United States"; "our understanding is that these United States citizens will not in the future be called upon by the Congolese government to engage in operational missions in the police action within the Congo."

UN Force Leaves Congo

4 years of UN military operations in the Congo were ended with the departure of the last UN forces June 30. UN Secy. Gen. U Thant, in a report to the Security Council, said that "the immediate outlook" for the Congo was "none too promising," but that the situation had been "greatly improved" since 1960 as a result of UN efforts. Warning that "failure to overcome present dangers would no doubt bring disintegration and ruin" to the Congo, Thant pledged continued UN technical assistance for the country. He told the Security Council that the UN could not continue its military operations past June 30 because the Congolese government had not requested that they be continued. He added that, in any case, extension of the UN military operations "would provide no solution to the remaining problems of the Congo." Congolese Pres. Kasavubu took personal command of the Congo's army as soon as the UN forces left, and the army assumed full responsibility for maintaining order.

Thant July 1 sent messages of thanks to the 34 nations that had provided troops for the UN's Congo operations. He reported that 126 UN troops had been killed in action in the Congo, that another 75 had died in accidents there and that 34 others had died of natural causes. Thant reported that the cost of maintaining the 20,000-man UN force had totaled $381,505,000. The cost of UN Congo civilian operations for the 4-year period was reported to be $51,545,015.

TSHOMBE HEADS NEW GOVERNMENT

Katanga Exile Replaces Adoula

Former Katanga Province Pres. Moise-Kapenda Tshombe and former South Kasai Pres. (self-styled king) Albert Kalonji ended their European exile and returned to Leopoldville June 26 and 27, respectively. The central Congolese regime had invited them to help establish and possibly participate in a new "reconciliation" government. Pressure was mounting to form a new government to cope with the revolts in Kivu, North Katanga and Kwilu Provinces. The regime was to be formed under a new constitution to be subject to formal approval by a national referendum.

Tshombe conferred first with Premier Adoula, Pres. Kasavubu, security chief Victor Nendaka and army chief Gen. Joseph D. Mobutu, then June 29 with Andre Lubaya, a founder of the Communist-backed National Liberation Committee, which was directing the Kivu and Kwilu revolts. Tshombe announced afterwards that Lubaya had pledged to support him "in all my actions, without condition." He said the committee had been "satisfied that my position in favor of the broadest possible reconciliation represents the only way of restoring the country to health." Tshombe said that Premier Adoula had given him "formal assurances" that imprisoned leftist leader Antoine Gizenga would be freed. Kalonji urged at a news conference June 28 the formation of a "national reconciliation" government by "a man about whom all the Congo can rally." He suggested that ministers "representing all the major factions" should assist the new premier.

Adoula resigned as premier on the expiration of his term June 30, but Kasavubu named him to head a caretaker government pending the formation of a new transitional regime.

Pres. Kasavubu asked Tshombe July 1 to explore the possibility of forming the new cabinet. Tshombe conferred July 2 with Antoine Kiwewa, leader of the moderate wing of the National Congolese Movement (the old Lumumbist party) and reported that Kiwewa had agreed to join in a "pacification campaign" to end the rebellions. Tshombe won Andre Lubaya's agreement July 3 to a joint statement affirming the National Liberation Committee's readiness to join a new government. Tshombe presented his program for a new government to Kasavubu July 4. The program advocated representation for all political groups.

Tshombe was designated premier July 6, his cabinet list was approved by Pres. Kasavubu July 8 and he formally became premier the following day. The new government was sworn in July 10. Tshombe held the posts of premier, foreign affairs minister and planning, foreign

trade and information minister. Kalonji was named agriculture minister, Lubaya health minister and Godefroid Munongo interior minister. Virtually all Congolese
factions were represented in the new cabinet, but real
power was believed to be concentrated in the hands of
Tshombe, Kalonji and Munongo.

The Tshombe regime July 16 released Gizenga from
the Congo River island on which he had been imprisoned
since January 1962. Gizenga pledged July 17 "to work for
pacification and reconciliation in the country." (But he
announced Aug. 28 the formation of an anti-government
United Lumumbist Party, to be "animated by the principles
of the national hero, Patrice Lumumba." He denounced
"the present de facto government," which, he said, "has
shown itself incapable of finding a political solution to the
country's problems.")

Kivu Province rebel leader Gaston-Emile Soumialot
complained in rebel-held Albertville July 18 that Tshombe's government was illegal and that Tshombe should
have consulted with "representative parties before forming his government."

Rebel Pressure Mounts

The new government was harassed by continued and
spreading revolt. Tshombe charged Aug. 1 that Communist China and several African states were supporting
the rebellion. He contended that the rebel National Liberation Committee was financed by the Communist Chinese
embassy in Brazzaville.

Rebel tribesmen attacked Stanleyville Aug. 3 and captured it Aug. 5. The Popular Army, linked to the National
Liberation Committee, led the rebel attack under the
command of self-styled Gen. Nicholas Olenga.

Tshombe conferred Aug. 8 with Count Charles de
Kerchove de Denterghem, Belgian ambassador to the
Congo, who reportedly suggested that the Congo regime
appeal to other African states for troops to help put down
the uprisings. But Tshombe declared at a news conference
Aug. 9: "We have no need for troops from the outside. We
have plenty of our own soldiers who can handle the situ-

ation. All we need is equipment." He reiterated that "some African states themselves are behind the troubles we have here."

Rebel tribesmen supported by the National Liberation Committee invaded Bukavu, capital of Kivu Province, in an attack from Shabunda Aug. 19. But government forces defeated them and complete control of Bukavu was gained Aug. 21 after a fierce battle in which at least 300 rebels were killed.

Tshombe appealed to UN Secy. Gen. Thant Aug. 20 to halt rebel infiltrations from the Congo Republic (Brazzaville) and Burundi. But Thant told newsmen that the UN could not legally resume any role in the Congo and that he had no knowledge of Peiping support for the Congo revolt. The Congolese government Aug. 21 began to deport thousands of citizens of the Congo Republic (Brazzaville), Burundi and Mali on the ground that their governments supported the revolt.

ACTION BEGUN AGAINST REBELS

U.S. & Belgium Expand Aid

U.S. State Undersecy. W. Averell Harriman conferred in Brussels Aug. 7 with Belgian Foreign Min. Paul-Henri Spaak on the deteriorating situation in the Congo. They reportedly agreed to expand U.S. and Belgian technical aid to the Congo.

4 U.S. C-130 transport planes carrying 3 helicopters and 105 U.S. military personnel (including 42 paratroopers) arrived in Leopoldville Aug. 13. The Defense Department explained that the C-130s, to be flown by Air Force pilots, were on "temporary assignment for transport functions" and were unarmed. U.S. Senate majority leader Mike Mansfield (D., Mont.) warned Aug. 21 that U.S. "involvement in the Congolese revolution" "may well lead to unsatisfactory consequences" for the U.S.

The ceding to the Congo of 3 Belgian bases—the Banana naval base and the Kitona and Kamina military bases—had been announced in a joint communique issued in Leopoldville Mar. 20 by Foreign Min. Spaak and then-Premier

Adoula. The base transfer was part of an agreement under which Belgium and the Congo divided responsibility for payment of the Congo's public debt, about $920 million in 1959, and Belgium turned over to the Congo about $740 million worth of stock it held in private Congolese firms.

Mercenaries Recruited

It was reported Aug. 22 that about 100 white South African mercenaries had been flown from Johannesburg in the past 2 weeks to Kamina in East Katanga Province to help the Tshombe regime fight the rebels. More mercenaries were being recruited. 30 mercenaries from several European countries were said to have arrived in Leopoldville Aug. 24. Several South Africans and Rhodesians were said to be participating in air missions against rebels in the Kasai area. The Congolese government Aug. 24 denied that it had recruited a foreign white mercenary force to fight the rebels. "We will fight the rebels with our soldiers," asserted Emmanuel Sinda, Tshombe's official spokesman. But mercenaries were reported to have been in the Congo for at least a month and to have received strong support from the U.S. and Belgium. Both nations were said to have contended at their August Brussels talks that mercenary units were needed to bolster the collapsing Congolese army and to lead effective resistance to the spreading rebellion.

South African Prime Min. Hendrick Verwoerd said Sept. 1 that he would limit the hiring of South Africans for the Congo force if the recruitment "got out of hand." "Large numbers of citizens and immigrants cannot be allowed to disrupt the labor market as a result of the spirit of adventure or for other reasons," he said. Tshombe asserted Sept. 4 that South African mercenaries "who come here on their own initiative will be sent home" and that "we have not called in South Africans to restore order." The hiring of white South African mercenaries ended Sept. 8. More than 1,000 South Africans had applied for the mercenary force, and about 250 actually reached the Congo.

Stanleyville Rebel Regime Formed

Rebels in the eastern Congo announced from Stanley-ville Sept. 7 the formation of a Congolese People's Republic aimed at overthrowing Tshombe's government. Christophe Gbenye, founder and head of the National Liberation Committee, was named president of the rebel government, and Gaston Soumialot was appointed defense minister.

(Congolese government troops, assisted by mercenaries, had launched an air and ground attack on Albertville Aug. 26 and recaptured it Aug. 30. Albertville had served as headquarters of the Revolutionary Government of the Eastern Congo, headed by Soumialot. Peiping denied Sept. 1 that it had intervened in the Congo revolt but acknowledged that it strongly supported the rebel movement.)

African Organization Acts

The Organization of African Unity (OAU), meeting in Addis Ababa, Ethiopia, took no action on requests by Tshombe Sept. 5 that other African nations send him troops and thus "enable me to dispense with" white mercenaries "whose presence in the Congo is embarrassing to us." He had made appeals to Nigeria, Ethiopia, Liberia, Senegal and Malagasy for troops, but had been rejected.

But the OAU Sept. 10 voted 26-0 to back a plan for ending the Congo rebellion under which: (a) a 10-nation commission led by Kenya Prime Minister Jomo Kenyatta would try to help the Congo reconcile opposing parties and try to mediate the Congo's dispute with its neighbors, particularly Burundi and the Congo Republic (Brazzaville); (b) "all those now fighting in the Congo" would "cease hostilities" and "all powers at present intervening in the internal affairs of the Congo" would desist; (c) the Congo would stop recruiting white mercenaries. Tshombe, who led his delegation at the OAU conference, said Sept. 10 that he would try to carry out the conference's resolution.

The OAU conciliation commission met in Nairobi, Kenya Sept. 18-22 to seek a means of halting the Congolese fighting. A commission communique said Sept. 20 that the group would meet with Congolese rebel leaders and visit the Congo (Brazzaville) and Burundi, the 2 nations accused by Leopoldville of aiding the rebels.

The commission appealed to the U.S. Sept. 22 to end all military assistance to the Congo and announced it would send a delegation of representatives from Kenya, Ghana, Guinea, Nigeria and the UAR to Washington to discuss the situation with Pres. Johnson. William Attwood, U.S. ambassador to Kenya, advised the commission Sept. 23 that the U.S. "could not agree to discuss" its "aid to the Congo without participation of the Congolese government, at whose request our aid is being given." Congolese Pres. Kasavubu assailed the OAU's proposed mission to the U.S. Sept. 23 as "manifest interference in the purely internal affairs of our country."

Tshombe Detained in Cairo

Tshombe was forcibly detained in Cairo Oct. 6-9 after he had flown to the UAR with a 50-member Congolese delegation to participate in the 2d World Conference of Non-Aligned Countries, which had opened there Oct. 5. Tshombe's trip was in defiance of a conference resolution barring him because of his alleged links with white colonialists and his presumed responsibility for the 1961 murder of the late Premier Lumumba. Tshombe was taken from the airport in Cairo and escorted to a government guest house, where he was placed under UAR armed guard. The Congolese government Oct. 6 sealed off the UAR and Algerian embassies in Leopoldville but was forced to lift the embassy blockade Oct. 8 after the UAR had made clear that it would detain Tshombe until it did so. Tshombe was released Oct. 9, and he left Cairo without attending the conference. Speaking to reporters in Paris later Oct. 9, he said the UAR's action had been dictated by its desires for "a weak and chaotic Congo" because a strong Congo might block UAR Pres. Gamal Abdel Nasser's plans "to dominate the African continent."

The final communique issued by the Cairo conference Oct. 11 denounced foreign intervention in the Congo as a "threat to neighboring countries," and demanded that the Tshombe regime halt recruitment of white mercenaries.

White Hostages Held in Stanleyville

Congolese rebel Gen. Nicholas Olenga informed Secy. Gen. Thant Sept. 2 that the rebels were holding about 500 white Europeans, most of them Belgians, as hostages in Stanleyville against possible Congolese government air raids. Olenga warned that his forces would fire on any approaching aircraft, including any UN planes, even if they carried medical supplies. He accused the UN, the International Red Cross and other agencies of an "imperialist plot" against the rebels.

Pres. Gbenye of the rebel Congolese People's Republic refused Sept. 15 to let a Red Cross mission bring food and supplies to Stanleyville's Europeans. He said that "we are at war" with the U.S., and he expressed "fear that the Americans through the channel of the International Red Cross would introduce themselves into the newly-liberated Congo." The rebels finally permitted a Red Cross plane carrying 4 doctors and 3 tons of medical supplies to land in Stanleyville Sept. 25, but the rebels emphasized Sept. 26 that no Europeans would be allowed to leave the city except those seriously ill or willing to promise to leave the Congo permanently.

A Congolese government force of 2,000 men, spearheaded by 400 white mercenaries, launched a major drive in early November to recapture Stanleyville. Anti-Castro Cuban exiles flying B-26 bombers were among the mercenaries. Starting their offensive from the Kamina base in North Katanga, the government forces, commanded by Col. Frederick van der Walle, a Belgian, captured Kibombo (280 miles south of Stanleyville) and Lueki (30 miles southeast of Kindu). 3 European hostages were executed by the rebels before they withdrew from Kibombo. Kindu and Ikela, a key road junction 180 miles from Stanleyville, were taken Nov. 6.

As the government troops overcame rebel resistance and gradually made their way toward Stanleyville, Gbenye declared in a broadcast Nov. 5 that U.S. and Belgian civilians behind rebel lines were being held hostages as "prisoners of war" in retaliation for "the bombings carried out by foreigners in liberated [rebel-held] areas."

U.S.-BELGIAN AIRDROP RESCUES HOSTAGES

Paratroops Retake Stanleyville

600 Belgian paratroops were dropped from U.S. Air Force transport planes near Stanleyville Nov. 24 on a mission to save the hostages held in the city by Congolese rebels. The paratroops recaptured Stanleyville the same day with the aid of Congolese government ground forces who were led into the city by 150 white mercenaries. Minutes before the city was seized, Congolese rebel troops marched some of the captive whites into the street from a hotel and machinegunned them. 29 hostages, including U.S. medical missionary Paul E. Carlson, 36, and Phyllis Rine, 25, who operated a Protestant hospital at Wasolo, were killed. But the paratroopers managed to save most of the other hostages due to the rebel troops' flight from the city. (Gbenye had disclosed Oct. 28 that Carlson had been arrested by the rebels at Yakoma Sept. 20 for "spying." Stanleyville radio had confirmed Oct. 25 that U.S. missionary William Scholten, accused of spying, had died Sept. 25; he reportedly had been beaten in a rebel jail at Aketi, 250 miles northwest of Stanleyville.)

The decision to go through with the paratroop operation had been approved by Pres. Johnson Nov. 23. The U.S. decision was reached in consultation with Belgium after U.S. and Belgian negotiators had failed to persuade the rebels to free the hostages. The rebels instead had become increasingly belligerent and had threatened to kill all the hostages on the spot if central government troops did not retreat from the Stanleyville area immediately. Reacting to the rebel threats, Belgium had ordered the paratroop force flown to Ascension I., a British possession in the South Atlantic, to prepare for deployment in the Congo if needed.

37 Americans, including U.S. Consul Michael P. E. Hoyt and his 4 staff members, were among the more than 500 hostages evacuated from Stanleyville to Leopoldville by U.S. planes after the rebel capital had been secured by the paratroop force. The U.S. and Belgium stressed Nov. 24 that the Stanleyville rescue operation had been

undertaken strictly as a "humanitarian" action. U.S. planes
and Belgian troops remained in the area temporarily to
protect other hostages outside of Stanleyville whose lives
were still threatened.

The Congo, the U.S. and Belgium informed the UN
Nov. 24 that their joint action had been the only possible
way to save the hostages' lives. Premier Tshombe said
in a note to Secy. Gen. Thant that he had authorized Belgium and the U.S. "to render my government the necessary assistance in organizing a humanitarian mission to
make it possible for these foreign hostages to be evacuated." Adlai E. Stevenson, U.S. ambassador to the UN, explained in a letter to Thant that the U.S. had "provided
air transport for a mission of mercy to effect the release
of over 1,000 civilian hostages from 18 nations, held in
and around Stanleyville" and that "the necessity for this
emergency rescue operation, carried out against threats
of mass executions, is illustrated by the murder of . . .
Carlson." Britain informed Thant that it had provided
Ascension Island airfield facilities for Belgian paratroops
"in the light of the humanitarian objective of this action."

The U.S.-Belgian rescue mission ended Nov. 28 when
the last plane, carrying 76 refugees, returned to Leopoldville. The Belgian paratroop force that had led the mission flew back to Brussels Dec. 1. At least 1,800 whites
and 300 Congolese had been rescued from rebel captivity
by the operation. There were, however, many expressions
of disappointment in Belgium and other Western countries
that many hostages were being left in rebel areas. Vis-
count Etienne Davignon, administrative chief of the Belgian Foreign Ministry, pointed out in Brussels Nov. 27
that no airfields existed in the rebel-held Bunia-Wamba-
Watsa region and it would have been impossible to liberate
hostages from there by plane; furthermore, the white
settlers in that section were scattered and difficult to
reach. U.S. officials claimed in Washington Dec. 1 that
the mission had been stopped for purely practical reasons
and not because of protests by other nations. Informing U
Thant of the completion of the operation Dec. 1, Stevenson
called on him to use his influence to obtain humane treatment of the hostages still in rebel hands.

U.S.-Belgian Action Protested

Soviet statements handed Nov. 25 to the U.S., British and Belgian embassies in Moscow denounced the landing of Belgian paratroops in Stanleyville as an act of "gross active intervention" and "a crime against the Congolese people." Algerian Pres. Ben Bella told a crowd of 10,000 in Algiers Nov. 25 that his government would continue to send "arms and volunteers to our Congolese brothers" [the rebels], "as we have already done." Ben Bella charged that "the unhealthy forces of imperialism, Belgian and American forces, are dealing a dirty blow to Africa." Tanzanian Pres. Julius K. Nyerere Nov. 26 assailed the U.S.-Belgian operation as an act "in defiance of the whole of Africa." A Communist Chinese government statement Nov. 27 expressed "great indignation" and strongly protested "the crime of aggression committed by the United States and Belgium" in the Congo.

Attacks on U.S., British and Belgian embassies and protest marches underlined the reaction to the rescue operation in many countries, especially those of the Soviet bloc. The U.S. embassy in Sofia, Bulgaria was stoned Nov. 25 by a mob of 400 led by African students and including Bulgarians and Chinese. A crowd of about 200, mostly Africans but including some Egyptians, attacked the U.S. embassy in Cairo Nov. 26 and burned both the adjacent U.S. Information Service's John F. Kennedy Memorial Library and the Marine guards' building. 41 demonstrators were arrested. A mob of 500 Africans in Nairobi, Kenya marched on the U.S. and Belgian embassies Nov. 26. The U.S., Belgian and British embassies in Prague were attacked Nov. 26 by at least 80 rock-throwing Africans. The U.S., Belgian, British and Congolese embassies in Moscow were attacked Nov. 28 by a mob of about 2,000, most of them African, Asian and Latin American students but including some Russians. Soviet police stood by during the height of the violence and intervened only after heavy damage had been inflicted. Soviet newsmen had appeared at the U.S. embassy to cover the incident shortly before the demonstration started. The Communist Chinese news agency Hsinhua reported that 700,000 persons participated in a Peiping rally Nov. 28 to protest U.S.-Belgian actions in the Congo. A mob of about 1,000 rock-throwing Indonesians, mostly students, attacked the U.S. Library and Cultural Center in Jakarta Dec. 4 in protest against American policies in the Congo. They burned or ripped about ¼ of the library's 15,000 books and tore down the U.S. flag and replaced it with an Indonesian one.

The OAU's Congo conciliation commission met in emergency session in Nairobi, Kenya and declared in a communique issued Nov. 28 that the commission "strongly condemns and protests" the role of the U.S., Belgium and Britain in the rescue of white foreigners in the Congo. The commission appealed for: (a) immediate withdrawal of foreign mercenary troops from the Congo; (b) a halt to "foreign military intervention"; (c) a truce between the central government and rebels; (d) a general amnesty for the rebels. (Tshombe, in Paris Nov. 30 to confer with French Pres. Charles de Gaulle, denounced the OAU's position on the Congo. He declared that the Belgian paratroops dropped on Stanleyville were "emergency troops whose actions were authorized by us for humanitarian purposes.")

Tshombe announced Dec. 4 that Congolese troops and white mercenaries had liberated 600 whites in rebel-held areas of the northern Congo since the termination of the U.S.-Belgian rescue mission. Mercenary troops Dec. 10 entered Yangambi, an agricultural research center 60 miles from Stanleyville, and rescued 59 whites held hostage by the rebels since September. Among those liberated were 32 priests and nuns, mostly Belgians, and staff members of the farm research unit. Mercenaries Dec. 29 entered the town of Wamba, 55 miles southeast of Paulis, and found 121 white hostages unharmed. 114 of the refugees, most of whom were Greeks, were flown to Leopoldville Dec. 30. They disclosed that the rebels had killed 30 hostages, most of them Belgians, in Wamba Nov. 26, the day Belgian paratroopers had landed in Paulis. William McChesney, a U.S. missionary, was among those slain. Their deaths brought to at least 153 the number of white hostages slain by rebels since Nov. 24.

(A UN official who recently had returned from Stanleyville reported in Leopoldville Dec. 6 that government authorities had rounded up thousands of suspected rebels in Stanleyville and were trying them by "acclamation" in the city's stadium. If the crowd jeered at an accused person, he was taken out and shot. 20,000 rebels were said to have been interrogated.)

UN Hears Complaint on Mission

The UN Security Council Dec. 1 received a 16-nation memorandum requesting an emergency session on the Congo. The note termed the U.S.-Belgian action in the Congo an "intervention in African affairs, a flagrant violation of the Charter and a threat to the peace and security of the African continent." By the time the Security Council opened debate on the issue Dec. 9, the complaint had mustered 21 Afro-Asian backers plus Yugoslavia.

Congo (Brazzaville) Foreign Min. Charles-David Gonao charged in the Security Council Dec. 9 that the rescue mission had caused "the massacre of scores of thousands of innocent blacks on the pretext of saving the lives of an insignificant number of whites." Ghanaian Foreign Min. Kojo Botsio asserted that Belgium, "after nearly a century of a system of political castration of the Congo" had "one way or another got . . . back" into the Congo. Malian Foreign Min. Ousmane Ba Dec. 10 assailed the Belgian-U.S. action as "a premeditated and coldblooded act" and a "murderous operation." Guinean Foreign Min. Louis Lansana Beavogui charged that Belgian, South African and Rhodesian mercenaries had "massacred hundreds . . . of defenseless Congolese civilians whom they have called rebels." Belgian Foreign Min. Spaak Dec. 11 condemned some of the Africans delegates' speeches as "painfully close to that type of racist feeling which has been so heatedly denounced and fought against."

U.S. Amb. Stevenson defended the rescue mission Dec. 14 as an act "to save the lives of . . . innocent people." Referring to African statements heard by the Council, Stevenson declared: "Never before have I heard such irrational, irresponsible, insulting and repugnant language in these chambers; and the language used . . . to contemptuously impugn and slander a gallant and successful effort to save human lives of many nationalities and colors." Nigerian Foreign Min. Jaja Wachuku said Dec. 15 that his government "does not find anything wrong with the Congo asking friendly countries to assist it in carrying out what the Congo thought to be a delicate operation that involved nationals of other countries, extricating them from what it believed to be a position that could not have brought credit to it." Soviet delegate Nikolai T. Fedorenko asserted Dec. 17 that Western "monopolies" were helping Congolese Premier Tshombe in a plot "to transfer the Congo to imperialists." Congo (Brazzaville) Foreign Min. Gonao declared Dec. 23 that the U.S. and Belgium "intentionally kept their nationals in the regions occupied by the Congolese rebels in order to have a pretext for intervention by military means." Stevenson Dec. 24 assailed Gonao's statement as "perhaps the most outrageous, the most despicable charge we have heard in this debate."

14 of the African complainants sought outright condemnation of the operation. The Council, by 10-to-0 vote (France abstaining) Dec. 30, approved a resolution urging a halt to all foreign intervention in the Congo, negotiation of a cease-fire there and the withdrawal of all foreign mercenaries. The resolution urged the OAU to seek a "national reconciliation" of all rival political factions in the Congo. The resolution, sponsored by Morocco and the Ivory Coast, did not specifically mention the Belgian-U.S. operation.

USSR, Africans Aid Rebels

It was reported from Cairo Dec. 6 that the USSR had agreed to finance and supply a joint UAR-Algerian military airlift to the Congolese rebels. Algerian and UAR Soviet-built AN-12 turbojet military transports were said to be flying Russian arms and ammunition from Algeria and the UAR to the Congolese insurgents via the Sudan. Ghana also was reported to be shipping arms to the rebels by this route. U.S. officials in Washington said Dec. 6

that at least one Soviet plane carrying military equipment for the rebels had landed in Khartoum in the Sudan. A report from Cairo said Algeria also was sending men to assist the Congolese rebels. The Algerian newspaper Alger Ce Soir said Dec. 7 that 3 Algerian planes had brought "food and medicine" to the Congolese rebels.

Premier Tshombe charged formally Dec. 7 that Algeria, the UAR and the Sudan were aiding the rebels. Tshombe said in a letter to Secy. Gen. Thant Dec. 24 that Egyptian and Algerian officers were leading Congolese rebel troops and that the Congo considered this a "veritable declaration of war." Gen. Joseph Mobutu, Congolese commander, said Dec. 15 that 10 Egyptian planes carrying ammunition and other military equipment had landed Dec. 14 in the Sudanese city of Juba and that the supplies were trans-shipped from Juba to the rebel-held border village of Aba. Mobutu said that 2 Algerian planes had landed in Juba the same day and that in the past few days a plane from Mali and 2 from Ghana had been seen there. He displayed what he said were Communist Chinese, Russian, Czech and German weapons and munitions discovered by Congolese forces in the retaking of Stanleyville.

THE CONGO AND ITS PEOPLES

THE CONGO AND ITS PEOPLES

(Adapted from U.S. State Department's 'Background Notes' series on foreign nations)

Geography

The Congo—now known as the Democratic Republic of the Congo—is located in the south-central part of the African Continent and covers an area of about 904,747 square miles. The Congo includes the greater part of the Congo River basin. It is landlocked, with the exception of a narrow strip of land on the north bank of the Congo which extends westward to the South Atlantic. It is bounded on the west and north by the Congo Republic (Brazzaville), the Central African Republic, and Sudan; on the east by Uganda, Rwanda, Burundi, Tanzania; and on the south by Angola and Zambia.

The central area of the Congo is a huge basin-shaped plateau sloping toward the west, covered by tropical rain forest. This area is surrounded by mountains on the west, plateaus merging into savannas to the south and southeast, and dense grasslands toward the Congo River in the northwest. It is bounded on the east by high mountains.

The Congo lies on the Equator and is generally hot and humid in climate. In the region south of the Equator the rainy season lasts from October to May, while north of the Equator it lasts from April to November. In the central region, however, rain falls more or less regularly throughout the year. During the October-May wet season storms are often violent but seldom last more than a few hours.

Peoples

The Congo has a population of 14,797,000 (June 30, 1962 estimate). Prior to independence, the non-African population totaled about 117,000. 75% of the whites were Belgians, and about 1,300 were Americans, most of them missionaries.

Congolese African ethnic groups have been estimated to number as many as 200 but the criteria for distinguishing these groups are not standardized. Despite this factor, the Congo's indigenous population commonly is divided into

3 major groups: Negroes, Pygmies and Hamites.

The Negroes form the bulk of the Congo's population. They are made up of the Bantu, who number approximately 9 million (the largest Congolese ethnic group); the Sudanese, estimated to number 2 to 3 million (found principally in the north and northeast areas of the country); the Nilotics, who are not numerous and live in the north.

The Pygmies are believed to have been the first inhabitants of the Congo basin. About 50,000 live in the western parts of the Congo and 30,000 in the Kibali-Ituri and Kivu districts.

The Hamitic population largely consists of Bahema shepherds living near the eastern frontier.

The Congo's African population is nearly evenly divided between Christians and adherents of either traditional religions or syncretic sects. There are approximately 4,000 Catholic and 1,000 Protestant missionaries in the Congo, operating perhaps 700 missions. The traditional religions vary widely among ethnic groups, and none are formalized. They embody such concepts as monotheism, animism, vitalism, spirits, ancestor worship, witchcraft, and sorcery. The syncretic sects are a mixture of Christianity and traditional beliefs and rituals. They often use Christian symbols and titles. Several which gained popularity in the 1920s sprang from Christian sources, and their prophets promised to lead people to a new way of life and a Black Christ. The most popular of these sects became a threat to law and order, and their activities were banned by the Belgian colonial administration. They have gained strength again since 1960 and, where they exist, tend to be identified more with radical political elements than with religion.

Languages

200 distinct African languages and dialects are believed to be spoken in the Congo. Although 4 of these are classified as major languages—Kingwana (Swahili), Lingala, Kikongo and Tshiluba—even they are regional in character and the total number of persons speaking any one of them constitutes only a small percentage of the Congo's total population.

Kingwana—commonly referred to as Swahili—is a dialect

of Kiswahili, introduced into the Congo by Arabs and especially the Zanzibari Swahilis in the course of 19th century slaving operations. It is spoken extensively in the northeastern, eastern, and southern regions of the country.

Lingala was developed in the 1880s in response to the need for a commercial language. In time the original fragmentary jargon was given written form, and it is now used extensively along the Congo River from Leopoldville to Stanleyville and in the north and northwest of the country.

Kikongo is the primary language of the narrow neck of territory betweeen Leopoldville and the ocean. A simplified dialect is spoken in the region just east of Leopoldville. Most of the languages of the western Congo belong to the Kikongo language group.

Tshiluba is the language of the Baluba ethnic group of Kasai. It is a form of the Kiluba language of the Kivu and Katanga Baluba and is widely used in the southeastern Congo.

French, introduced by the Belgians, is the only common language of the country. Although it is widely spread geographically, it is spoken only by those Congolese who have had some education. It is the official language of the country.

Governmental Structure

During the colonial period of the Congo's history, the Belgian Parliament had the supreme authority for making laws affecting the territory but it seldom exercised this function except to approve annual budgets. Actual legislative power was vested in the king and was executed by decrees made upon recommendation of the minister of the Belgian Congo and Ruanda-Urundi and of the Colonial Council. The minister was appointed by the king and was a member of the Belgian Cabinet. He was president of the Belgian Colonial Council, which was composed of 14 members, 8 of whom were appointed by the king, 3 chosen by the Senate, and 3 by the Chamber of Representatives. This body passed on legislative measures pertaining to the Congo and considered matters referred to it by the king.

The Congo was divided into six provinces: Leopoldville, Equator, Oriental, Kivu, Kasai, and Katanga. (After independence the Congolese Parliament altered the provincial structure to comprise 21 provinces plus a capital district centered on the city of Leopoldville.)

The king and the Belgian government were represented in the Congo by a governor general appointed by the king with the advice and consent of the Belgian Parliament. Prior to independence there were no strictly elective bodies, although in 1957 voting took place in 3 cities for municipal councilors, subject to official confirmation. Administrative jurisdiction was exercized (in descending order) by the governor general, 6 governors of provinces, 18 commissioners of districts, and 123 administrators of territories. A consultative Government Council met annually.

In May 1960, the Belgian Parliament enacted the bill which provided the basic governmental structure for the independent Congo. This act, the Fundamental Law, served as the constitution of the Congo until June 30, 1964. The Fundamental Law did not greatly alter the structure of government as it had existed when the Congo was a colony. However, significant additions were made. Under the Fundamental Law a parliamentary form of government was provided for. At the national level Parliament consisted of a Senate and the equivalent of a House of Representatives. The executive was a prime minister, chosen by Parliament, and a president. All members of the national and provincial parliaments were chosen in national elections.

A constitutional commission, made up of representatives of social, political, and regional groups, convened in January 1964, to draw up a permanent constitution for the Congo. The new consitution was submitted to a plebiscite, reportedly was approved by 90% of those responding, and was promulgated on August 1, 1964. The new constitution provided for a modified presidential form of central government. The position of prime minister was retained, but real executive power was given to the president.

Economy

In the years just before independence the Belgian Congo had become the most developed country in tropical Africa. In the period 1950-57 it achieved an annual growth rate in real terms (constant prices) averaging 6.7%.

The growth rate declined with a drop in primary product prices in 1957 and with a sharp rise in the burden posed by the volume of borrowing needed to continue a high rate of expansion. Nevertheless, some 60% of the $2.5 billion in investments in the Congo during the 1950s originated in the private sector, overwhelmingly in the form of reinvestment. By the end of the 1950s the Congo possessed the highest wages and the highest literacy rate in tropical Africa, produced 8% of the world's copper and most of the world's cobalt and industrial diamonds, and was credited with a vigorous and competitive agriculture.

In 1959 the Congo (including Rwanda-Burundi) attained a commercial surplus of $192 million (exports $500 million, imports $309 million). Even in 1964, despite the decay of native agriculture, the abandonment of plantations, losses through smuggling, and the decline in its export prices, the Congo was exporting at an estimated $312 million annual rate.

The Congo's manufacturing facilities are well developed by African standards. Even before independence the Congo produced more than 90% of its beer, soap, and cigarettes; 80% of its needs in cement and sacks; 60% of its paint and shoes; and close to 50% of its cotton fabric and blankets. The Torre report prepared for the European Economic Community stated that the Congo's index of industrial production in 1962 was 19% above 1958, while the rise in the Leopoldville metropolitan area was 40%.

Congolese agriculture is considered to be relatively efficient. In contrast to their privileged position in the former British and French territories, planters in the Congo did not enjoy sheltered preferential markets or price supports and were forced to compete with the most efficient world producers.

Improved techniques raised palm oil production from 500 to 3,100 kilos per hectare. In the case of rubber, the substitution of new strains quadrupled the past yield, while coffee yields, which were 250 kilos per hectare in 1927, were as high as 1,575 kilos on better plantations in 1957. Comparable increases in productivity occurred in other crops, among them cocoa, rice, corn manioc, cotton and bananas.

The Congo suffered a decline in export earnings during the

early years of independence, due partly to the secession of
Katanga and South Kasai, whose combined mineral production had represented almost half the country's earnings,
but also to the sharp decline in the export of crops dependent on individual native planters. Plantation agriculture
was not as troubled by the unrest, but many exporters were
discouraged by the declining real value of the Congolese
franc as recurrent budget deficits bred inflation.

The reintegration within the Congo of South Kasai in the
fall of 1962 and of Katanga in January 1963 helped restore
much lost earning power, and the value of the country's exports for 1963 reached 88% of the level for 1958, the last
normal pre-independence year. The pattern of foreign trade
also changed. The U.S. share of the Congo's imports rose
from 14.7% in 1958 to 31.2% in 1963, but the increase was
due to AID and P.L. 480 (agricultural surplus) programs.

A major monetary reform introduced in November 1963
devalued the Congolese franc from 65 to the dollar to a new
split rate of 150 to 180. The devaluation encouraged exports
and the production of domestic food crops, while the government exchange tax (derived from the split rate) sharply reduced the budget deficit. Living costs were stabilized during
the second quarter of 1964.

U.S. aid given directly to the Congo, or to the United
Nations for technical assistance and peacekeeping activities
in the Congo, totaled over $400 million by the end of fiscal
1964.

INDEX

A